Edith Wharton

Revised Edition

Twayne's United States Authors Series

Joseph M. Flora, Editor

University of North Carolina, Chapel Hill

TUSAS 265

Edith Wharton

Revised Edition

Margaret B. McDowell

University of Iowa

Twayne Publishers
A Division of G.K. Hall & Co. • *Boston*

Edith Wharton, Revised Edition
Margaret B. McDowell

Copyright 1991 by G. K. Hall & Co.
All rights reserved.
Published by Twayne Publishers
A division of G. K. Hall & Co.
70 Lincoln Street
Boston, Massachusetts 02111

First Edition © 1976 G. K. Hall & Co.

Copyediting supervised by Barbara Sutton.
Book production by Gabrielle B. McDonald.
Book design by Barbara Anderson.
Typeset in Garamond
by Compositors Corporation, Cedar Rapids, Iowa.

First published 1990.
10 9 8 7 6 5 4 3 2 1

Library of Congress Cataloging-in-Publication Data

McDowell, Margaret B.
     Edith Wharton / Margaret B. McDowell. — Rev. ed.
         p.   cm. — (Twayne's United States authors series ; TUSAS 265)
     Includes bibliographical references and index.
     ISBN 0-8057-7618-4
     1. Wharton, Edith, 1862–1937—Criticism and interpretation.
  I. Title.   II. Series.
PS3545.H16Z745   1990
813'.52—dc20   90-43605
                                                                        CIP

To my husband, Frederick P. W. McDowell

Contents

Preface

A revision of this study is necessary, in part, because of the amount, range, and originality of recent Edith Wharton scholarship and criticism. The publication by R. W. B. Lewis of *The Collected Stories of Edith Wharton* (1968) and the Pulitzer prize–winning *Edith Wharton: A Biography* (1975), with the subsequent opening of the Edith Wharton papers at the Beinecke Library, Yale University, generated this new biographical and critical interest in Wharton. Lewis's biography enables us to see Wharton fully as a human being and artist, and he corrects the somewhat distorted view of Wharton's personality as that of the arrogant, jealous, and prudish woman that Percy Lubbock presented in *Portrait of Edith Wharton* (1947). Professor Lewis and Nancy Lewis have provided further materials for understanding Wharton's life and work with their editing of *The Letters of Edith Wharton* (1988).

Shortly after the publication of Lewis's authorized biography, Cynthia Griffin Wolff published what might be called a supplemental biography focusing on Wharton's conscious and subconscious. Wolff had read the Lewis biography in part in manuscript and had been conducting research in the notebooks, diaries, and other papers to further her view that these materials would illuminate the understanding of Wharton's mind and that Wharton's books reflect developments or regressions in her psyche at certain points in her life. In *A Feast of Words: The Triumph of Edith Wharton* (1977) Wolff argues convincingly that a terror-ridden childhood had deeply scarred and inhibited Wharton. To a degree that view challenges the statements on the book jacket for her 1934 autobiography, *A Backward Glance*: "*A Backward Glance* tells the story of a secure and happy childhood. . . . She was too serene to be vindictive. Readers who savor old wounds and old hatreds will be disappointed." Indeed, Wharton's autobiography is quoted here as saying, "a bruise to the soul . . . life puts a quick balm on it, and it is recorded in a book I seldom open." Wolff believes, as a result of her psychological research, that Wharton's fear of her unsympathetic mother, who lived to 1900, caused her to suffer sexual repression from which her affair with Morton Fullerton in middle age began significantly to liberate her. Wolff alleges that, as a result of this affair, Wharton for the first time was able to write openly about sexuality in her fiction—unsuccessfully so, according to Wolff, in *The Reef* (1913) and successfully in *The Age of Innocence* (1920). Wolff's book has encouraged a number of other scholars to apply to Wharton theories of developmental psychology promulgated by Freud and Erik Erikson.

Elizabeth Ammons in several articles and in her excellent book *Edith Wharton's Argument with America* (1980) related Wharton's fiction to social history and feminist politics. With much insight, Ammons interprets the novels and stories as expressing Wharton's understanding that in America patriarchal power has limited the lives of women from all classes, although she thinks—more than I do—that Wharton turned far away from this concern in her later years. Like Cynthia Wolff, Judith Fryer in *Felicitous Space* (1986) considers the relationship between Wharton's fiction and the portrayal of women in graphic art at the turn of the century. Younger scholars have recently written on the neglected works of the 1920s and 1930s—especially *The Children* (1927), the four novellas comprising *Old New York* (1924), the early novellas *The Touchstone* (1900) and *Sanctuary* (1903), and the travel books. Alfred Bendixen, Kristin Lauer, and Margaret Murray are continuing their important bibliographical work. The increased availability of the Wharton manuscripts and working notebooks at Yale has furthered studies of Wharton's style and her processes of composing and revision—for example, articles on *The Age of Innocence* by Alan Price and by Joseph Candido.

A highly significant force in the Wharton revival has been the growth of the Edith Wharton Society under the early leadership of Annette Zilversmit, the editor of the *Edith Wharton Newsletter* and a critic whose interest in psychology and myth, especially in Wharton's fiction, is notable. So also has been the work of the Edith Wharton Restoration (under the direction of Thomas Hayes and Scott Marshall), which includes the restoring of Wharton's beloved home, the Mount, and her walled gardens as a tribute to her achievement. Dramatizations of several short stories by Wharton have been performed on the grounds in recent summers, and educational tours are conducted regularly. A significant conference of Wharton scholars took place at The Mount in 1987.

My revision of *Edith Wharton* is designed to reflect the new wave of Wharton scholarship and to express some new understandings of Wharton's life and works that I have achieved over the past fifteen years.

I owe much to my husband, Frederick P. W. McDowell, for his criticism of my manuscript at various stages and for his shared appreciation of the works of Edith Wharton. I am also much indebted to my friends in the Edith Wharton Society, particularly R. W. B. and Nancy Lewis, Annette Zilversmit, Alfred Bendixen, Kristin Lauer, Margaret Murray, Katherine

Joslin, and Alan Price, as well as to many others whose devotion to Wharton scholarship has given me invaluable encouragement. Annis Pratt's understanding of my earliest feminist criticism of Wharton was a source of strength to me, and her exhaustive research continues to be helpful. I thank the Graduate College of the University of Iowa for providing me with a research assistant, and I am most grateful for Joyce Meier's assistance in that capacity.

Edith Wharton, 1905. *Photograph courtesy of the Edith Wharton Restoration.*

This photograph of Edith Wharton was taken in 1905. Though sometimes captioned "Christmas 1905," it was probably taken in autumn. *The House of Mirth*, published 14 October 1905, ran serially in *Scribner's* for eleven issues, January to November of that year. The first edition of 40,000 copies had been succeeded by several editions by Christmas when over 140,000 were in print; the book remained the nation's best-seller for several more months. In a 11 November letter to Charles Scribner she writes, "It is a very beautiful thought to me that 80,000 people should want to read *The House of Mirth*, and if the number should ascend to 100,000 I fear my pleasure would exceed the bounds of decency. . . . And by the way, I hope you got that photograph I sent you about ten days ago, with my eyes down, *trying to look modest*?! The photographer swore he would send it off punctually, but I have my doubts, as he hasn't sent me one yet" (*The Letters of Edith Wharton*, ed. R. W. B. Lewis and Nancy Lewis [New York: Charles Scribner & Sons, 1989], 95). Henry James wrote from Lamb House, 18 December, to thank her "for the so handsome photograph in which you *baissez les yeux* so modestly before the acclamations of the world. They are all transcribed for you. . . . I surely make out, in that compendium you are reading, so that you look thoroughly in possession of your genius, fame, and fortune. It is a very charming picture, as charming, that is, as a picture can be, which doesn't none the less, 'do you justice.' But I take it gratefully for my *étrennes* and place it, ever so conspicuously among quaint tributes already beginning to cluster on my mantel shelf" (*Henry James Letters*, vol. 4, ed. Leon Edel [Cambridge, Mass., and London: Harvard University Press, 1984], 384).

Chronology

1862   Edith Newbold Jones born 24 January in New York City to George F. and Lucretia Stevens Rhinelander Jones.

1866–1872   Travels in Europe with parents.

1872–1879   Spends winters in New York, summers in Newport, Rhode Island.

1877   Writes novella *Fast and Loose* (published 1937).

1878   Debuts, Fifth Avenue, New York. *Verses* privately published.

1880   Travels in France and Italy with parents and Henry Stevens.

1882   Father dies in March; engagement to Stevens announced in August, broken in October.

1882–1885   Lives with mother in New York and Newport.

1883   Attracted to Walter Berry, Bar Harbor, early summer; to Edward Wharton, Newport, late summer.

1885   Marries Teddy Wharton. Spends winter and spring in Italy, summer in Newport.

1888   Charters yacht to cruise Aegean for three months. Receives inheritance from her grandfather's cousin.

1889–1891   Publishes two stories and three poems. Writes "Bunner Sisters," a novella published in *Xingu* in 1916.

1893   Buys Land's End, Newport. Paul and Minnie Bourget visit.

1894–1898   Suffers serious depressive illness.

1897   Publishes *The Decoration of Houses*, written with Ogden Codman.

1899   Publishes *The Greater Inclination*, a collection of stories.

1900   Publishes *The Touchstone*, a novella.

1901   Publishes *Crucial Instances*. Builds The Mount, Lenox, Massachusetts.

1902   Publishes *The Valley of Decision*; *Es Lebe das Leben*, titled by Scribners' *The Joy of Life*, translation from German of

Hermann Sudermann's tragic drama. Corresponds with Henry James.

1903   Publishes *Sanctuary*, a novella. Teddy Wharton suffers mental illness.

1904   Publishes *The Descent of Man and Other Stories* and *Italian Villas and Their Gardens*. Henry James visits The Mount. Purchases the first of many automobiles.

1905   Publishes *Italian Backgrounds* and *The House of Mirth*. Dines at White House after inaugural of Theodore Roosevelt.

1907   Publishes *Madame de Treymes* and *The Fruit of the Tree*. Whartons and James tour France by car. Rents Vanderbilt apartment in Paris for two winters. Teddy's illness worsens. Edith enters Fullerton affair.

1908   Publishes *The Hermit and the Wild Woman* and *A Motor-Flight through France*. Visits Henry James in London.

1909   Publishes *Artemis to Actaeon*. Begins friendship with Bernard and Mary Berenson.

1910   Publishes *Tales of Men and Ghosts*. Edward Wharton enters Swiss sanatorium. Edith moves to 53 Rue de Varenne, Faubourg Saint-Germain in which she resides until 1920. Walter Berry moves from Cairo to Paris.

1911   Publishes *Ethan Frome*. Whartons separate permanently, and The Mount is sold.

1912   Publishes *The Reef*, which marks Wharton's shift from Scribner's to Appleton.

1913   Publishes *The Custom of the Country*. Her divorce, followed by travels in Germany with Berenson. Starts never-completed novel to be called "Literature."

1914   Travels in Africa with Percy Lubbock and Gaillard Lapsley. Is in Majorca with Berry when World War I begins. In Paris organizes refugee workrooms, hostels, and hospitals.

1915   Publishes *Fighting France*. Visits front lines with Berry.

1916   Publishes *Xingu and Other Stories* and *The Book of the Homeless*. Cares for over six hundred Belgian orphans. Henry James dies.

1917   Publishes *Summer*. Awarded Order of Leopold by Belgium.

Made member of French Legion of Honor. Travels three weeks in Morocco as guest of French government and of Resident General Hubert Lyautey of Morocco.

1918   Publishes *The Marne*. Buys Pavillon Colombe, eighteenth-century house twelve miles north of Paris in village of St. Brice-sous-Forêt.

1919   Publishes *French Ways and Their Meaning*. Leases and restores Sainte Claire, a medieval convent above modern Hyères on the French Riviera, as winter home.

1920   Publishes *In Morocco* and *The Age of Innocence*.

1921   Awarded Pulitzer Prize for *The Age of Innocence*.

1922   Publishes *The Glimpses of the Moon*, a best-seller.

1923   Publishes *A Son at the Front*. Becomes first woman to be awarded honorary doctorate of letters by Yale University.

1924   Publishes *Old New York*. Is first woman awarded Gold Medal of the National Institute of Arts and Letters.

1925   Publishes *The Mother's Recompense*; *The Writing of Fiction*.

1926   Publishes *Twelve Poems* and *Here and Beyond*. Charters yacht for ten weeks and repeats Aegean cruise of 1888.

1927   Publishes *Twilight Sleep*, a best-seller. Walter Berry dies.

1928   Publishes *The Children*, a best-seller. Teddy Wharton dies.

1929   Publishes *Hudson River Bracketed*. Suffers serious illness. Awarded Gold Medal for "special distinction in literature" by the American Academy of Arts and Letters. Invited to receive honorary doctorate at Columbia University, but must cancel trip because of illness.

1930   Publishes *Certain People*.

1931   Revives friendship with Morton Fullerton.

1932   Publishes *The Gods Arrive*. Visits Rome.

1933   Publishes *Human Nature*.

1934   Publishes *A Backward Glance*. Travels in Holland, Scotland, and England. Again invited to Columbia University to receive honorary degree but has to decline because of political problems in France.

1936   Publishes *The World Over*.

1937   Dies August 11 after a stroke and is buried in the Cimetière
        des Gonards at Versailles next to ashes of Walter Berry.
        Leaves papers to Yale University with stipulation that publi-
        cation be withheld for about thirty years. *Ghosts* published
        posthumously with dedication to Walter de la Mare.

1938   *The Buccaneers*, though unfinished, is published and edited
        with an afterword by Gaillard Lapsley, her literary executor.

Chapter One
Edith Wharton: Woman and Artist

Edith Wharton is probably the most distinguished woman writer of fiction America produced before World War II. During a career of almost fifty years, she wrote fourteen full-length novels, thirteen novellas, eleven short story collections, nine nonfiction books, three small volumes of poetry, and many magazine articles and reviews. She won a Pulitzer Prize for *The Age of Innocence* (1920), was the first woman to receive an honorary doctorate of letters from Yale University (1923), and was decorated for her war relief work by the French government with the Cross of the Legion of Honor (1916). She was the first woman awarded the Gold Medal of the National Institute of Arts and Letters (1924), and she also received the Gold Medal of the American Academy of Arts and Letters (1929).

Edith Wharton's relatives came from old New York families whose names Washington Irving had mentioned in his accounts of Hudson River history. They were mostly well-to-do merchants, bankers, and lawyers, although by the time of Wharton's birth many of them lived on their inheritances. Men of their class indulged in sea fishing, boat racing, and hunting, while women—including Lucretia Rhinelander Jones, Wharton's mother—found themselves preoccupied with lavish dinner parties, ritualized calling days, and the replenishment of their fashionable wardrobes.

Wharton's parents, to cope with the inflation that followed the Civil War, lived and traveled in Europe for much of the time until Edith was ten. Knowing five languages by that time, the child largely educated herself through her reading and divided her time between summers at Newport (where neighbors included the Vanderbilts) and winters in a house on Fifth Avenue in New York City. Just before her fifteenth birthday in 1877 she completed the thirty-thousand-word novella *Fast and Loose,* not printed until 1977. In her late adolescence she again spent two years in Europe with her parents as her father's health failed; for part of this time Harry Stevens, to whom she was engaged, accompanied her.

In her fiction Wharton treated the aristocrats of old New York with mingled respect and satire. As she asserted in her autobiography, *A Backward*

1

Glance (1934),[1] they upheld high standards in education, exemplified good manners, and observed "scrupulous probity" in business and private affairs. She chronicled and reflected upon the demise of this small aristocracy in the novellas in *Old New York* (1924), in a few short stories such as "After Holbein," and in her novels *The House of Mirth* (1905), *The Age of Innocence,* and *The Buccaneers* (1938).

In *A Backward Glance* she reveals the positive facets of her early life: a sensuous response to nature and to architecture, a love of books, a fascination with the creation of stories, an immersion in her aristocratic milieu, and an excitement in travel. But she adds that as a child she had an ability to see the ugly details of life alongside the beautiful, and she had also a concern for the powerless and inarticulate. All these elements that defined her childhood manifested themselves in her adult life and work as well. They account for the great breadth and variety of her fiction, as well as for its basic unity, which is provided largely by the themes and unresolved questions that reappear in her works.

An overview of Wharton's life necessarily includes her unhappy forty-year relationship with her mother, her twenty-eight-year marriage troubled by unresolved sexual dissatisfaction and intellectual and cultural differences, her chronic illnesses, and her husband's worsening mental illness after 1903. These factors account in part for her postponed commitment to a professional writing career, despite her early interest in writing fiction. Of unusual importance to her and to her writing were her many long-term friendships with both men and women, her homes, her artistic and social milieu in the United States and in France, and her unquenchable thirst for travel. Her early nonfiction books—*The Decoration of Houses* (1897), *Italian Villas and Their Gardens* (1904), and *Italian Backgrounds* (1905)—reflect these interests and form an integral part of both her later fiction and nonfiction.

In the summer of 1883 Wharton renewed and intensified her relationships with two family acquaintances—first, in July at Bar Harbor, Maine, with Walter Van Rensselaer Berry, a twenty-four-year-old law student in Washington, D.C., who had graduated from Harvard two years earlier and spent a year traveling in Europe; and later in the summer in Newport, with Edward "Teddy" Wharton, a thirty-four-year-old member of a prominent Boston family and a friend of one of her brothers. In this summer Wharton was still grieving for her father, who had died in March 1882, and she was also recovering from the humiliation of her broken engagement to Harry Stevens, caused by his mother's objection to a difference in the status of the two families. The engagement had been announced in the Newport *Town Topics* the previous August with a tentative marriage date set for the middle of October 1882. On 28 October, however, *Town Topics* announced that the marriage was "postponed, it is said, indefinitely." The Newport *Daily News* reported that "The only reason assigned for the breaking of the engagement hitherto existing between Harry Stevens and Miss Edith Jones is an alleged preponderance of intellectuality on the part of the intended bride. Miss Jones is an ambitious authoress, and it is said that, in the eyes of Mr. Stevens, ambition is a grievous fault." R. W. B. Lewis points out that Mrs. Paran Stevens did not have to relinquish her son's share of his father's estate until he reached twenty-five or was married. Because her son was twenty-three at this time, the broken engagement permitted her to control his million and a quarter trust fund another two years.[2]

Walter Berry strongly attracted Wharton, but when he returned to Washington she lost contact with him for fourteen years. After a few weeks, Teddy Wharton began to court her. The result was their engagement by March 1885 and wedding on 29 April of that year. Before they married, they checked with a physician who assured them that the mental illness in Edward's family was unlikely to recur in his life. Teddy Wharton was affectionate, playful, and generous. A good host, he made Edith's many friends comfortable in their home. Consummation of the marriage was postponed, and it appears that the couple never achieved satisfying sexual expression with each other. Perhaps related to this problem, Wharton's asthma attacks worsened, and she suffered depression that caused years of nausea. Following a decade of marriage, she entered a program of psychiatric care in Philadelphia, similar to the regimen advocated at the time by S. Weir Mitchell. A few years after her recovery, her husband's depression and related illnesses worsened—notably after 1903—and he never recovered, although he lived another twenty-five years. Complications resulting from his illness made an eventual divorce inevitable. Just before the dissolution of the marriage and when Edith was on her way to England, Edward Wharton sold The Mount in Lenox, the home and grounds Edith loved and had helped design. (In her last years she wrote that love of this residence made it unbearable for her ever to revisit it.) Subsequently, in 1911 she became a permanent resident of France, and her divorce decree on the grounds of Teddy's adultery became final in 1913. When Teddy Wharton died in 1928, Edith remembered him with nostalgia and kindness, describing him in a letter to Judge Robert Grant as "the kindest of companions till that dreadful blighting illness came upon him." Later, in *A Backward Glance,* she mourned "his sweetness of temper and boyish enjoyment of life which struggled long against the creeping darkness of neurasthenia" (*BG,* 326).

In 1897, fourteen years after drifting away from Edith, Walter Berry had again moved into her life as a frequent visitor at The Mount, and until his death in 1927 he was her chief literary adviser and close friend. They traveled together and shared reading, love of art and the theater, and mutual friends. Berry had graduated from Harvard in 1881 and had traveled in Europe for a year before reading for the law in Washington in 1882 and 1883. From 1908 to early 1911 he served as judge of the International Tribunal in Cairo; during this time Edith saw him less often but ordinarily sent him her manuscripts before she submitted them to a publisher. Over a thirty-year period he continued to edit her work carefully and to choose the stories he thought she should include in her short story collections. His influence on her career was undoubtedly great, although she contended that he never interfered with the "soul" of her writing. From 1917 to 1923 he was president of the American Chamber of Commerce in Paris. She and Berry lived in apartments in the same building in the Rue de Varenne until 1920. When she moved after restoring a summer home in St. Brice and a winter home above modern Hyères, Berry moved into the apartment that had been her residence for a decade. They were traveling in Majorca when World War I broke out—a time when Henry James romantically likened them to George Sand and Frédéric Chopin.

Like Wharton, Berry knew several languages and was an insatiable reader. She considered him a fine literary critic but felt that his emphasis on the analytical had kept him from developing into a fiction writer. At his death she was overcome with grief, recording in her diary, "The stone closed over all my life." In *A Backward Glance* she also celebrates his lifelong influence over her inner life in these statements of tribute:

Whatever I saw with him, in the many lands we wandered through, I saw with a keenness doubled by his, and studied afterward with an ardor with which his always kept pace. (*BG,* 117)

I cannot picture what the life of the spirit would have been to me without him. He found me when my mind and soul were hungry and thirsty, and he fed them till our last hour together. It is such comradeships, made of seeing and dreaming, and thinking and laughing together, that make one feel that for those who have shared them there can be no parting. (*BG,* 119)

Although Berry remained her literary mentor longest, she had several other such mentors who were also her good friends and supporters. She recalled late in her life the debts she owed both William Brownell and Edward Burlingame, her editors at Scribner's; Brownell's friendship was primarily that of a correspondent while Burlingame became "a devoted personal friend." The elderly Professor Charles Eliot Norton of Harvard, whose daughter Sara was Wharton's close friend, assisted her with research into eighteenth-century Italy for her first novel, *The Valley of Decision* (1902). Paul Bourget, a French novelist and essayist, along with his wife, Minnie, maintained a close relationship with Wharton from 1893 to his death in 1935. He insisted that she must, at the beginning of her career, give up her "frivolity" and associate with people who "think and create." The Bourgets introduced her to Parisian intellectual and artistic circles. They encouraged her in her writing as she and Teddy traveled with them in Italy in 1899 collecting material for her first novel. Paul Bourget engaged his young associate, Charles du Bos, for the translation into French of *The House of Mirth*, which led to an early interest in her work in France. After the war, Wharton became the neighbor of the Bourgets at Hyères. In *A Backward Glance* she recalls Paul Bourget as "one of the most stimulating and cultivated intelligences I have ever met, and perhaps the most brilliant talker I have known" (*BG*, 123). For over forty years Bourget discussed Wharton's ideas and writing with her.

Bourget was important in arranging the initial contacts between Wharton and her most famous mentor, Henry James, at the turn of the century. When the Whartons attended a dinner party with Henry James in late 1887 and another in Venice in 1891, Edith lacked the courage to converse with him. In 1889 he wrote to the Bourgets about his impressions of her first collection of short stories, *The Greater Inclination,* commenting that he thought she had chosen for the collection the best of her stories with which he was familiar. He thought the ones she chose to reprint revealed herself, whereas the lesser ones showed "another person." He was probably referring to himself and implying her imitation of him in the less original stories that she had rejected. James wrote to Wharton in autumn 1900, after she sent him her story, "The Line of Least Resistance." He advised her to write about American life. Again in 1902 he wrote her a long letter praising *The Valley of Decision* but insisting that she "Do New York!" In December 1903 he called on the Whartons in London; he wrote appreciatively to her after reading her third collection of stories, *The Descent of Man,* printed in May 1904, and the Whartons called on him at Rye the same month. During his first American visit since 1883 (the one that formed the basis of his book *The American Scene*), James called on the Whartons at The Mount in October 1904, in New York at New Year's, and again at The Mount in the summer of 1905. In 1908 he spent two weeks with them in Paris during his first visit to the Continent since 1899. In 1911 he was at The Mount comforting her in the weeks just before she decided finally to divorce and to take up permanent residence in France. After James renounced his American citizenship early in the war and as his health began to fail, Edith Wharton visited him to offer her comfort, and in the last days of his life in 1916 she was in touch daily with his nurse. Their letters to one another in times of illness and grief are poignant, but more important was their ability to laugh at the same things. They had, Wharton remarked, "a sense of humour or irony pitched in exactly the same key" (*BG,* 173). His "elaborate hesitancies," so annoying to many, were to her "a cobweb bridge . . . an invisible passage over which one knew that silver-footed ironies, veiled jokes, tiptoe malices, were stealing to explode a huge laugh at one's feet" (*BG,* 178). She recalls him reading Walt Whitman in a crooning voice, "his voice filled the hushed room like an organ adagio," and then they talked of the poet, "tossing back and forth to each other treasure after treasure" (*BG,* 186). At times, her energy appalled him, and he referred to her as "deranging and desolating, ravaging, burning and destroying." Although her mature artistry is only minimally Jamesian, their friendship was vital for both, and their criticism of each other's work stimulating. Both writers were interested in their craft as writers, and both believed, as James expressed it in "The Art of Fiction," that "Art lives upon discussion, upon experiment, upon curiosity, upon variety of attempt, upon the exchange of views and the comparison of standpoints. . . . The successful application of any art is a delightful spectacle, but the theory too is interesting."[3] Both would have agreed with her statement in *The Writing of Fiction* (1925) that a writer is obliged to speculate about his craft even though his inspiration can never be rationally defined: "if no art can be quite pent-up in the rules deduced from it, neither can it fully realize itself unless those who practice it attempt to take its measure and reason out its processes."[4] One sees other similarities between them in reading James's prefaces to the New York edition of his work, all written during the years of their friendship. He uses as pervasive themes the relationship between art and life, the relationship between the artist and his art, and the relationship between the artist and his life. With Wharton, exploration of these themes dominates her early stories: in *Crucial Instances* (1901) five of her seven stories center on artists. Outlines, abortive versions, and letters to her publishers indicate that for thirty years she planned to write a novel called "Literature" that would trace the growth of a literary artist. From these false starts there grew finally *Hudson River Bracketed* (1929) and *The Gods Arrive* (1932), two related novels about Vance Weston's struggle to become a successful literary artist and a human being who can in the end reach beyond self-concern through his own suffering as he recreates it in his fiction. Wharton and James both used the novella, both developed international themes in their narratives about Americans, both wrote ghost stories, both experimented with various uses of irony, both sought for precision in style, and both frequently reflected the incidents of a narrative through a central consciousness.[5] James was more than a literary mentor to Wharton. When he died, her sense of loss was profound: "His friendship was the pride and honor of my life."

Although Wharton's career as a widely recognized novelist begins in 1905 with *The House of Mirth,* she had by then already achieved recognition for three volumes of short stories, three nonfiction books, and two novellas. The stories had clearly linked her with James because of their epigrammatic quality and stylized dialogue, although they are more direct than his and they develop a dramatically compressed situation rather than a meticulously elaborated one. The novellas, *The Touchstone* (1900) and *Sanctuary* (1903), show less sophistication and control than do her short stories, although her more Jamesian *Madame de Treymes* (1907) would soon link her work in the genre of the novella with that of James.

In this early period, her nonfiction had revealed her sophistication as a scholar, her versatility, and her love of art, history, and nature. The printed copies of the first edition of *The Decoration of Houses* were exhausted immediately, as was the English edition. In *Italian Villas and Their Gardens* she concentrated on plantings rather than houses, providing descriptive notes for the famous gardens in Maxfield Parrish's illustrations. She also included details on the dimensions of shrubs and flower beds and on the effects to be achieved by variations in levels, patterns of shade and light, and curves. The book at once became a manual for architects and landscape gardeners, and she regretted that the publishers had not allowed her to include scale drawings for the houses and gardens. In *Italian Backgrounds* she describes in loving detail the impressive monuments she had observed while working on *Italian Villas.* Both these books anticipate the informal, colloquial quality of all her travel books, despite her habitual use of scholarly detail and historical allusion.

Edith Wharton's first novel, the two-volume *The Valley of Decision,* centers on the conflict between an individual's need for freedom and his inevitable loss of some of that freedom in an ordered society—one of her recurrent themes. She called the book "not . . . a novel at all, but only a romantic chronicle" (*BG,* 205). This chronicle, laid in eighteenth-century Italy, first presents the development of Odo Valsecca from his childhood among the peasants through his adolescence and the loss of religious conviction as a result of his learning. His study of philosophy causes him to embrace for a time the political and metaphysical ideas that brought about the French Revolution. To finance reforms in his duchy when he comes to power, he marries the rich widow of another duke and makes Fulvia, who is the woman he loves and the daughter of his professor, his mistress. After a mob kills Fulvia, as a supposed witch, Odo becomes increasingly reactionary and eventually opposes political change of any kind. In the end, the revolutionaries, whom he had helped, overthrow him as a tyrant intent on preserving the old order.

Edith Wharton's love of the Italian landscape and her immersion in eighteenth-century Italy are evident throughout this novel, especially in the vivid details that are assimilated in the action and the characters. Her extensive research included such projects as making lists of the perfumes that a duchess might have used and of the most popular lap dogs among the Italian gentry. Odo's reactions to specific philosophical theories and to art history as he studies with his professor undoubtedly reflect Edith Wharton's own enthusiasms. Perhaps Odo's wistful skepticism when he goes to mass in the cold dawn in order to recapture a lost religious fervor reflects her own incertitude as a young woman.

Reaction to the novel was mixed. Theodore Roosevelt never forgave his friend for failing to have Odo marry Fulvia. One anonymous reviewer who typified the "genteel" aversion that some of Wharton's early critics felt toward her sexual frankness and religious skepticism declared that "no refined woman would be willing to associate her name even with the condemnation of it." Generally, however, the reception was enthusiastic, with reviews describing it as "a classic," as "giantlike," and as "the most splendid achievement of any American man or woman in fiction." Charles Eliot Norton, who had helped her in her research, wrote to Samuel G. Ward that her book was "a unique and astonishing performance and . . . places Mrs. Wharton among the foremost of the writers in English today." Years later, in 1952, Van Wyck Brooks declared that "in power of . . . imagination . . . few novels could have greatly surpassed it." He also contended she had gone beyond her famous mentor, Norton, in her feeling for Italian Post-Renaissance Art.[6] These estimates are excessive; for, though the book is brilliant in places and its characters have life, Wharton was not yet able to sustain imaginatively a book of this length. In none of her later fiction did she again reach farther into history than her parents' generation.

Wharton's first novel was followed three years later by *The House of Mirth,* which established her as an American novelist of notable stature. Within two months, the novel broke records for sales; Wharton had become a celebrity. Her literary career was assured.

A second period of remarkable artistic development and personal growth, between 1907 and 1913, parallels a period of emotional tumult in her life. A central figure in this experience provided a different kind of friendship and mentoring than that offered earlier by Charles Eliot Norton, Walter Berry, Paul Bourget, and Henry James. In the spring of 1907, in Paris, Edith Wharton fell in love with Morton Fullerton, an American journalist employed in the Paris office of the London *Times*. He was a former Harvard student of Charles Eliot Norton and friend of Sara Norton. By January 1908 the relationship had become a sexual one.[7] Fullerton made a trip to the United States in October 1907 during which he not only visited Wharton at The Mount but went also to Bryn Mawr where he became informally engaged to his cousin, Katherine Fullerton—at least in Katherine's understanding. Katherine, who had grown up in his household, had loved him since childhood but had learned only in 1903 that she was not his sister. Katherine came to Paris in the fall of 1909, when Edith was in England, and Fullerton visited her in Bryn Mawr on occasion, but he neglected to write her for long periods of time despite her almost daily, impassioned letters to him. In the same years Wharton endured similar neglect from Fullerton that alternated with times of intense sexual fulfillment with him. In 1910 Katherine poured out her heartbreak in a two-thousand-word letter to Fullerton, which he may have failed to answer. She broke the engagement and soon after married a medieval scholar, George Gerould. Katherine Fullerton Gerould, under that name, became a well-known writer of fiction, whom Edith Wharton assisted in getting published and reviewed with praise.

Only gradually did Wharton learn of the complexities of Morton Fullerton's life, although by 1890 he was a friend of the Nortons, Paul Bourget, and Henry James and, like her, an acquaintance of Theodore Roosevelt. During 1903–4 Fullerton was married to an actress and singer, Camille Chabert; their daughter was four when he met Edith Wharton. He divorced Chabert on the grounds that she had damaged his reputation by accusing him of having mistresses, and she had to pay court charges for the divorce, according to R. W. B. Lewis's research.

Fullerton had indeed supported a mistress, referred to as Madame Mirecourt, for an undetermined number of years both before the marriage to Chabert and during it. When he later sought to withdraw from the relationship, Mirecourt threatened blackmail, and Fullerton corresponded with Henry James in late 1907 about his anxieties. As a gesture perhaps of quixotic generosity, Wharton in 1909 conspired with Henry James and Fullerton's publisher to have some of her funds anonymously transferred to him to enable him to "pay off" the vindictive woman. Even so, as late as 1914

Wharton wrote to Fullerton, admonishing him to support his aged parents rather than to continue paying this woman a "lifetime" pension.

Fullerton was particularly vulnerable to scandal because he was bisexual and because his partners included wealthy and well-known figures. For example, from 1890 to 1893 he had had a three-year affair with Margaret Brooke, ranee of Sarawak, who had borne her husband, the white rajah, seven children before she returned from the British colony with her three surviving sons and became involved with Fullerton. Her letters suggest her fear that, as a middle-aged woman of high social position, she would appear foolish and subservient if the affair were revealed. Fullerton's affair with Ronald Gower, a noted sculptor and, like Fullerton, a former friend of Oscar Wilde, would have made him vulnerable to blackmail if the relationship were to have become widely known.

Although Wharton continued to write to Fullerton from time to time even into her seventies, the letters after 1911 are cordial but lack passion. They are businesslike, with a few playful remarks on occasion. The earlier letters reflect the depth of her emotion for Fullerton, as does the diary she saved for her literary executor, an action that contrasts with her probable destruction of her letters to Walter Berry immediately after his death. This "love diary," recorded from 29 October 1907 to 12 June 1908, implies that from the beginning she recognized the Fullerton affair as inevitably evanescent.[8] She longs to be to him "like a touch of wings brushing by you in the darkness, or like the scent of an invisible garden that one passes by on an unknown road." In the diary, she confesses bewilderment at Fullerton's behavior. When he angers her, she finds inexplicably that her love for him increases. Her sense of humiliation emerges when she acknowledges that love for him has destroyed her pride and independent identity. Several entries express her hope that their meetings can take place in secluded and romantic settings and that the sexual embrace can become an intellectual and spiritual communion as well— expectations that in general were frustrated. It is difficult, therefore, to understand this affair as liberating, as some critics have.

By 1908 Wharton's letters to Fullerton reveal an extremely low sense of self-worth, and she is confused about who she is.[9] Typical are her descriptions of herself in "Sunday Early April 1908" (*Letters,* 138–39) as "tiresome and impossible," "not-worth-giving-another-thought-to," "numb dumb," and "not worthy to write to or to think about." Repeatedly, in referring to his harshness or neglect in this letter and others that followed in spring and summer 1908, she expresses herself in such terms as "paralyzed," "stunned," or "drove me straight back"—all suggesting emotional effects as strong as those of physical violence. If she complains, she quickly apologizes and takes the blame upon herself in a subservient manner. Like the typical long-abused or neglected woman in any society, she apparently found it easier to accept humiliation for some years than to risk losing her lover. Actually, Wharton was perhaps unconsciously reflecting in her own life the sufferings of some of the women in her slightly earlier fiction who had retreated into similar passivity and self-denigration. One thinks especially of Justine Brent in the last half of *The Fruit of the Tree* (1907) and possibly even of Lily Bart. Fortunately, Wharton had enough independence and knowledge of her own abilities to allow her to declare in letters to Fullerton that a woman like herself deserved something better and to acknowledge in "Thursday Mid-April 1910" (*Letters*, 208) that her life had been better before she knew him. In a letter she wrote 17 May 1908 (*Letters*, 145) she even criticized his lovemaking because he did not let her savor fully the ecstasy following a moment of "perfect nearness" but instead left her "to feel that I have like been a 'course' served and cleared away!"

Wharton acknowledged, however, that the extreme intensity of the affair had been a "gift" for which she was thankful. In a letter written 26 August 1908 (*Letters*, 160–62) she recalls that Fullerton had once said that she "should write better for this experience of loving," and she felt this judgment to be true. Her full experience of physical love during these years undoubtedly enlarged and deepened her writing. In her previous fiction, for over fifteen years she had been exploring questions of marriage, adultery, and male domination. Her actual experience now catches up with her vivid imaginative and vicarious renditions of impassioned love, of the agony involved in the renunciation of love, and of the disappointed expectations in intimate relationships.

The first evidence of this ability to connect her strong feelings and conflicts during the affair with her art appears in her sequence of eight sonnets, "The Mortal Lease," written in autumn 1908 and published in *Artemis to Actaeon* (1910). Arline Golden traces the influence of George Meredith's *Modern Love* on Wharton's "The Mortal Lease,"[10] and we know that Wharton was poring over Meredith's fifty-sonnet sequence that fall when Henry James insisted that she accompany him on a visit to Meredith. We know also from the love diary that she was moved by Fullerton's interest in Meredith's poetry. In their formal conventions, the sonnets mask only to a degree the personal nature of Wharton's outpouring of joy and misgiving. Like Wharton, Meredith's husband/narrator wishes that love were immortal and that it could be deeply spiritual as well as physical. Several of Wharton's sonnets employ a dialogue device, which can be interpreted as an argument either with Fullerton or with her other self. The sonnets recognize that their love has an elemental nature in "monster-haunted mud," but they also celebrate its highest spiritual reaches in her assertion that the lovers need not "forego the deeper touch of awe / On love's extremist pinnacle."

Some of the other love poems in *Artemis to Actaeon,* written prior to the Fullerton affair, explore themes similar to those in "The Mortal Lease"— sorrow that love is evanescent, concern that love should be both spiritual and physical, distress that a woman cannot be for her lover both the "nymph that danced on Illysus" and the "nun entranced / Who night-long held her Bridegroom in her soul," and conviction that security, honesty, trust, and responsibility are essential in love.

Nevertheless, the passion intensifies and the argument enlarges in the verses that Wharton wrote during and after her affair. One sees emotion deepen in the poems written in the spring of 1909, when simultaneously she came under influence of John Donne, Walt Whitman, and Meredith. Intensity of expression within the restraints of poetic form dominates "Colophon to 'The Mortal Lease,' " written in June. In "Colophon" (three parts, forty-two lines) she expresses postcoital sadness in sensing that her ecstasy had not been shared by her lover. In "Ogrin the Hermit," Ogrin shelters the lovers Tristram and Iseult, who have escaped from her husband, King Mark. Ogrin daily converses with Iseult to persuade her to give up her lover, but her defense of freedom in love as more ancient and elemental than Christian tenets persuades him to bless her even as she returns to the prison of her marriage. In "Terminus," comprised of fifty-two long, Whitman-esque lines, the poet thanks her lover for their night at the Charing Cross hotel near the railroad station in London. But the joy and vigor of love diminishes as she meditates in their dingy room on the many other lovers who have slept where she and her lover have and on the many ghostly figures in the predawn darkness calling farewell as they board trains that move down steel rails beyond the city and eventually to the graveyard. The dinginess of the room affronts her. The realization of possible loss, separation, ugliness, and death in this poem undoubtedly reflects Wharton's own insecurities in her troubled affair.

In Wharton's stories written during this period, "The Letters" and "The Choice" seem related to the affair with Fullerton. In "The Letters," published in 1910, a woman overlooks her sudden discovery years later of an insult: her husband's failure to open impassioned letters that she had written him daily for years before their marriage. In refusing to acknowledge openly this revelation, she feels she is acting on a newly attained wisdom. In "The Choice," written in 1908 but not published until 1916, Wharton emphasizes the remorseless dilemma of a wife who must choose between husband and lover, with the realization that one man will die symbolically when she chooses the other or when fate takes the choice out of her hands.

The influence of her love affair with Fullerton is notable also on some of her longer fiction. In *The Reef* (1912) Wharton presents with insight (that probably only her tortured love for him could have given her) the equally tortured relationship of her genteel heroine Anna Leath with Darrow, a man who loves her but who had been unfaithful to her during their engagement. Anna doubts the integrity of Darrow—perhaps even unreasonably, while she also envies Sophy Viner for the passionate nights that she had enjoyed with her "stolen" lover. The juxtaposition of love and suffering in this novel and in *Ethan Frome* (1911), *The Custom of the Country* (1913), *Summer* (1917), *The Old Maid* (1924), and *The Children* (1928) all reflect in some degree the intensity that Wharton gained from direct sexual experience as well as some of the ambivalence she experienced in love from 1907 to 1911. Rose Sellars's dilemma in *The Children* parallels that of Anna Leath, but her greater leaning toward reason rather than passion makes her a somewhat less sympathetic character than Anna Leath is. In *The Reef, The Children,* and *The Age of Innocence* Wharton succeeds in engaging the reader's sympathy for all three characters in the love triangles present in the books, something she was unable to do earlier in *The Fruit of the Tree.* While readers were accepting more freedom in sexual behavior, Wharton also reflects her greater sophistication about sexuality, adultery, and marriage in these later fictional relationships, and this sophistication also affects the technique and tonal characteristics of the later fiction. In *Twilight Sleep* (1927) for example, Wharton's greater understanding of sex not only sharpens the cynicism that underlies her satire; it also provides the human warmth and appeal that lighten the novel somewhat.

Charles Eliot Norton, Paul Bourget, Henry James, Walter Berry, and Morton Fullerton were the friends and mentors who most influenced her work between 1900 and 1911. About the time Wharton became a permanent resident of France in 1912, she added to them two new and significant friends, Bernard and Mary Berenson. Berenson was a widely known American art critic, theoretician, dealer, and writer of influential books, especially on Italian Renaissance art, and Mary, his Quaker wife, assisted him in his work, as did Nicky Moriano, who also became Wharton's friend. They are part of a new stage of growth in Wharton's life and work that began about 1911 when her divorce went forward, when she became an expatriate, when Teddy sold The Mount, when her passion for Fullerton cooled, and when Berry left Cairo to live in Paris, where he was to become the president of the American Chamber of Commerce. At this time Wharton was preparing

Ethan Frome and *The Reef* for publication and was making progress on *The Custom of the Country* after considerable delays.

At the beginning of this period of Wharton's life as writer, she and Walter Berry traveled in Italy in the fall of 1911 and spring of 1912, in Sicily in the spring of 1913, and in Spain and Majorca in the summer of 1914. She also took automobile trips with Berenson in Germany in the summer of 1913 and with Percy Lubbock and John Hugh Smith, younger British friends, in Tunisia and Algiers in the spring of 1914. In spite of her extensive travels, her recurrent asthma, and her personal anxieties, she succeeded just before the war in publishing *Ethan Frome, The Reef,* and *The Custom of the Country.*

Because of the advent of war in 1914, Wharton's writing of fiction came to a standstill for almost three years. *Xingu and Other Stories* (1916) contained only one recently written story. It does, however, include two significant first publications: "The Choice," the self-revealing story written in 1908 and described above, and "Bunner Sisters," the novella Wharton had written in 1891–92. Although she had regularly collected her stories in books since 1889, no new collection appeared between 1916 and 1926. In 1917 she published *Summer,* a novella set far away from the war both in time and place, and in 1918 came *The Marne,* a novella about a young American fighting for France, in which she fuses a realistic treatment of battle with the supernatural.

When Wharton returned to Paris in the fall of 1914, after a brief residence in England, many Parisians and the government offices had already moved to Bordeaux.[11] At this time the Red Cross and government agencies, occupied with their work at the front, assigned the care of refugees to volunteers behind the lines. One of these was Charles du Bos, who ten years before had translated *The House of Mirth.* He organized a relief project, first called the Accueil Franco-Belge and later the Accueil Franco-Américain, with Wharton as head of the American committee and Elisina Tyler as her chief aide. Other people associated with this enterprise were Royall Tyler (until he became a lieutenant and later a major in the U.S. Army, interrogating German prisoners of war); Mary "Minnie" Cadwalader Jones, divorced wife of Edith's brother, who carried out her assignments in America; Anna Bahlmann, Wharton's German teacher in adolescence and her secretary for most of her career; and Walter Berry, who helped with funding and problems of wartime communication through his office at the Chamber of Commerce and his understanding of international law. Wharton grieved in late 1915 as Anna Bahlmann died of cancer about the same time that Egerton Winthrop died and Henry James, who had recently given up his

American citizenship because of the United States' failure to enter the war, suffered a massive stroke.

In offices near the Champs-Élysées, from nine in the morning to midnight, the volunteers distributed meal tickets, clothing, and information about lodgings. The organization comprised ten units: a workroom for a hundred seamstresses (who made, among other things, lingerie marketed in America), an employment agency, a furniture store, a restaurant, a food distribution center, a hospital, a dental clinic, an isolation ward, and four sanatoriums. By 1918 this organization was caring for five thousand refugees in Paris and four colonies of old people and children in rural areas and had acquired four sanatoriums for the tubercular. When the Belgian Ministry of the Interior in 1915 appealed to Wharton on behalf of six hundred and fifty orphans, she established the Children of Flanders Rescue Committee, calling the project her "most appealing charity." In six homes she housed seven hundred and fifty children and one hundred and fifty nuns and elderly people. Interested in the new motion picture industry, she made and sent films of the children to America for Minnie Jones to use in fund raising. During the war the center lodged thirty thousand refugees, found work for eight thousand, and treated one hundred thousand military personnel suffering from tuberculosis. In addition to her daily work at the center, Wharton at night wrote letters to raise funds and to encourage America's entry into the war, and she tried to make each letter a personal one. Contributions came from New York, Boston, Philadelphia, and Paris, largely as a result of her efforts.

If Wharton's war work interfered with her writing of fiction, she succeeded both in her public activities and in the writing of nonfiction. In *Fighting France, from Dunkerque to Belfort* (1915), a collection of articles already printed in *Scribner's,* she describes the trips she took under military authorization to deliver supplies to hospitals in battle areas and to observe their activities. The book contrasts sharply with the pleasure trip across France that she had earlier covered in *A Motor-Flight through France* (1908). In another travel book, *In Morocco* (1920), she recounts the journey made in 1917 to Morocco with Walter Berry as honored guests of General Hubert Lyautey and the French government. *French Ways and Their Meaning* (1919), also a collection of magazine articles already printed, includes sympathetically drawn vignettes of French villagers and others, though the book is disorganized and she makes some ill-considered judgments about American women as compared with French women. Wharton's trips behind the lines to military hospitals provided the milieu for *A Son at the Front* (1922), in which the hero's parents get permission, first, to search for their wounded son and then to stay for several days with

him in his field hospital. In *The Book of the Homeless* (1916) she compiled
the works that writers, musicians, and artists had donated to the cause. Igor
Stravinsky provided a musical score; Max Beerbohm, Claude Monet, Jean
Renoir, and Auguste Rodin gave illustrations and paintings; Sarah
Bernhardt and Eleonora Duse furnished letters; and Joseph Conrad, John
Galsworthy, Thomas Hardy, William Dean Howells, Henry James,
George Santayana, and William Butler Yeats contributed essays, poems,
and fiction. Theodore Roosevelt wrote the introduction, and Wharton
translated all the materials not written in English. For these many tireless
activities, the president of France in 1916 decorated her with the Cross of
the Legion of Honor.[12]

After the war, Wharton began in 1918 to remodel the eighteenth-century
Pavillon Colombe in St. Brice outside Paris, and in 1920 she moved from the
apartment in the Rue de Varenne that had been her home for ten years. By
then she was also restoring an ancient monastery at Hyères, where she spent
her winters for the rest of her life. It was near the homes of her old friends the
Bourgets and Ogden Codman. Her health had been damaged by the rigors
of her wartime relief activities and, at fifty-six, she was exhausted. She postponed writing *A Son at the Front,* a decision that may have interfered with its
reception four years after the war was over, when stories of war seemed less
timely.

The Age of Innocence ranks with *The House of Mirth* and *The Custom of the
Country* as a masterpiece. Here she again registers, as in the other two novels,
the interplay of her characters with the society that produced them and with
which they must come to terms. *The Age of Innocence* has for milieu the old
New York that her parents knew, and the four novellas published in a set as
Old New York (1924) also have a nineteenth-century setting. Her last and unfinished novel, *The Buccaneers* (1938), has a similar evocative historical
background in the 1860s.

The Age of Innocence won the Pulitzer Prize in 1921 over Sinclair Lewis's
Main Street. Ironically, Wharton's friendship with Lewis began at this time
when she apologetically wrote to him.[13] Lewis, in turn, dedicated his next
novel, *Babbitt,* to her.[13] Since his college days, he had assiduously studied her
fiction and now visited her in France. In *Hudson River Bracketed* Wharton satirically recounts the awarding of a "Pulsifer Prize" to a mediocre writer, an indication perhaps that she took the honor lightly and disliked the imputation
that she had received the prize by default because some judges saw her novel
as more wholesome than Lewis's. In 1923 Wharton became the first woman
to receive an honorary doctorate of letters from Yale or at any major American university. In 1924 she won the Gold Medal of the National Institute of

Arts and Letters for "distinguished service," the first woman to be so honored. In 1929 she received the Gold Medal of the American Academy of Arts and Letters for "special distinction in literature." In 1929 Columbia University invited her to receive an honorary doctorate and again in 1934. Both times she had to cancel plans to travel to New York because of illness.

In spite of these awards and honors and in spite of the fact that her novels of the 1920s became best-sellers, she began to lose esteem among some critics, who complained that she had lost touch with the contemporary American scene and that she did not fully understand the working class and the facts of poverty. The adverse judgments perplexed and hurt her, and on 9 June 1925 she revealed some chagrin and self-doubt in a letter to a childhood friend, Margaret (Daisy) Chanler. She wondered why she, as "the priestess of the Life of Reason should take such things to heart. . . . [B]ut as my work reaches its close, I feel so sure that it is either nothing or far more than they know. . . . And I wonder a little desolately which" (*Letters*, 483).

If her novel *The Glimpses of the Moon,* written for the *Pictorial Review* as a serial and published in 1922, is disappointing and dull, it nevertheless became a best-seller in both America and England and a popular 1923 film. *The Mother's Recompense* (1925), written for the same magazine, presents a believable character, Kate Clephane, a divorcée who had left America with her lover twenty years before in disgrace. The novel fails to some degree, however, because Kate's situation on her return to her country is a strained one. She lacks the courage—or cruelty—to tell her daughter, Anne, that she had been a few years earlier abandoned as the mistress of Chris Fenno, who is now Anne's fiancé. The reader cannot tell where Wharton stands on Kate's decision, or perhaps Wharton herself was confused. In *Twilight Sleep* Wharton experiments with satire and presents exaggerated characters from a shallow upper-middle-class society, a mode she had used far more brilliantly in *The Custom of the Country.* Its weaknesses notwithstanding, *Twilight Sleep* became the top best-seller for 1927 in the United States and often blends a poignant sympathy with her satire of American women. In 1928, *The Children,* a satire on upper-class, much-married- and -divorced people who seek pleasure on the Riviera and neglect their children, earned more money for Wharton than any book she had earlier written. Critics were less enthusiastic than the general public, but in the late 1980s this novel received substantial attention from Wharton scholars.

Hudson River Bracketed and *The Gods Arrive* became Wharton's substitute for her long-postponed and never-completed "Literature" begun in 1913. Despite many arresting pages, both books are marred by strident satire. Subjects of her ridicule include the midwestern small town (here named Euphoria, Illinois, where Vance Weston grows up and is inspired to become a novelist), superficial literary cliques in New York and Paris, exploitative editors, new trends in the writing of fiction that appeared in the 1920s and 1930s, and American tourists abroad. Vance Weston fails to convince as a character of intellectual and artistic potential, but his grandparents and most of the women are incisive creations. These women include Vance's angry aunt, his naive first wife, the mistress who will bear his child after the second novel ends, and his blowsy childhood sweetheart, who becomes a tycoon.

In Wharton's last years her writing activity was varied, and much of it was of high literary quality. She renewed her interest in ghost stories and, just before her death, wrote one of her finest achievements in the genre, "All Souls." She collected her best stories of the supernatural in *Ghosts* (1937) and dedicated the book to Walter de la Mare, whom she recognized as a kindred thinker and an important artist preoccupied with the supernatural, although they had apparently never met or corresponded. *The Buccaneers,* even as a fragment that Gaillard Lapsley sought to complete according to her plans, showed great artistry, and some of her best short stories appeared in this last decade of her life.

Chapter Two
"Sharpening of the Moral Vision":*The House of Mirth*

The House of Mirth, Edith Wharton's first best-selling novel, marked a turning point, she said, in the control of her craft because she learned from writing it the importance of systematic daily effort in sustaining the intensity of her imagination. To meet an emergency at Scribner's, she agreed to print five chapters immediately and to supply the rest of the novel in installments within six months. At age forty-three, she experienced for the first time the ambiguous stimulus of writing under pressure of deadlines. She said in *A Backward Glance* that, as a result of her sustained engagement with *The House of Mirth,* she began to understand how to write a novel. In beginning this novel she hoped to make it unlike her romantic chronicle *The Valley of Decision,* but she feared that she lacked the "constructive power to achieve anything beyond isolated character studies, or the stringing together of picturesque episodes" (*BG,* 205). In *The House of Mirth* she first wrote a novel (as she had already written novellas and short stories) with economy and concentration, focusing upon one central character and confining herself to a few important themes.

Lily Bart as Victor and Victim

In *A Backward Glance* Wharton speaks of the importance of an author's deep gaze into the chosen subject and her own doubts about her choice of fashionable New York in *The House of Mirth* as a suitable subject for such probing. But she decided that a trivial subject, such as fashionable New York society, could gain "dramatic significance" through what it destroyed—in this case the young, beautiful, and spirited Lily Bart, who descends from a position of aristocratic prestige and glamour to anonymity and poverty. Wharton also saw that an author must "extract from such a subject the typical human significance which is the story-teller's reason for telling one story rather than another" (*BG,* 206–7). Such human significance comes in this novel from the less visible drama enacted *within* the character of Lily. This second theme of the book derives from Lily's gaining a degree of moral or spiritual victory through suffering apparent defeat in a society that lacks meaning and direction and through her returning good for evil. The novel thus balances in its construction Lily's steady movement toward tragedy and her far less consistent movement toward understanding of herself and others, a process that eventually reveals that she is in essence an individual superior to those who had formerly represented to her all the social graces.

Wharton wrote in 1906 to Erskine Steel that her thesis for this novel was to be found near its close in the paragraph that begins, "It was no longer, however, from the vision of material poverty that she turned with the greatest shrinking."[1] The paragraph emphasizes that Lily's death results primarily from solitude, from being "uprooted," from never having a place, community, or family that could give her some "center of early pieties, of grave enduring traditions." This interpretation of her destruction as deriving from a vulnerability to loneliness and from an alienation related to modern individualism leads Richard Poirier in his analysis of *The House of Mirth* to conclude that as a novel of manners it is more closely related to the novels of George Eliot and Jane Austen—who respected old pieties—than to the exhaustive psychological preoccupations of Henry James.[2]

In her sprightly talk with Lawrence Selden in his lodgings at the beginning of the novel, Lily complains—only half comically—of the attractive options men have. Selden, she says, does not need to rush to marry before age thirty or be thrown on the rubbish heap. He can wear a coat that is growing "shabby" and still be invited to dinner. A woman, she claims, is required to buy fashionable clothes until she drops and if she cannot afford them she must "go into partnership" with a rich man. Her complaints are real, but she treats them humorously because ("leaning back in the luxury of her discontents") she generally accepts the pleasure-loving and highly materialistic society that is the only world she has known since birth.

Selden stands at a distance from her, assessing her, regarding her body as if he were examining an expensive work of art for possible purchase. He observes separately her "vivid" head, the waves of her auburn hair, her braids, her little ear, her eyelashes, the tint of her skin, and her hand "polished as a piece of old ivory" beneath her sapphire bracelet. Amused and judgmental, he enjoys her chatter and finds her "amazingly pretty" and "at once vigorous and exquisite, at once strong and fine." He even considers her as he thinks of his mother's portrait, "charming and graceful . . . all smiles and Cashmere." But he wonders whether Lily—eleven years past her coming out—has what his mother taught him to want: "character in a pretty woman." He admits to himself that he is not interested in a "nice" girl, and it is common knowledge that he has just had a two-year affair with the married Bertha Dorset.

On the other hand, Selden's idealistic talk impresses Lily, but she fears marriage to a man who, like herself, has come from an aristocratic and debt-ridden family and has no living parents. He is anxious about her love of pleasure and money, although he knows only people who love pleasure and money; and he fears the gossip that suggests she associates mostly with newly rich people and may not observe scrupulously all the stipulations of the old codes of propriety. Nevertheless, almost all the warmth in the novel comes from the hesitant, timid, and anxious encounters between these two people.

Throughout Book 1 Lily dutifully pursues rich candidates for marriage and does so with zest and humor as well as with misgivings and cynicism. Skillfully, she attracts millionaires, but just as they are about to propose marriage, she flees or impulsively offends them. Her destruction by this society begins slowly in Book 1, but becomes relatively precipitous in Book 2. Early in the novel the staid aristocrats (the Gryces, Penistons, Stepneys, Van Alstynes, and Van Osburghs) accept her and view her as being by birth one of them. But she finds life with these people constricting. Searching for pleasure and a wealthy mate, she seeks another group, the rich and powerful leaders of high society (the Trenors, the Dorsets, Ned Silverton, and Carrie Fisher), who welcome her because of her youth, beauty, and charm. She tries to keep up with these wealthy acquaintances as she moves from house party to house party.

Gus Trenor, Lily naively assumes, has invested a pittance for her that is to pay huge dividends. Only much later does she learn that, in exchange for the "dividends" he has been giving her, he had expected sexual favors. He lures her at night to his empty townhouse, closed for the winter, informs her that she owes him nine thousand dollars, rages that she knew from the beginning what he expected, and blocks her access to the door. By steady control of her fear and anger in this violent encounter, Lily escapes rape, but throughout the rest of her life she suffers from the irrational shame that rape victims often feel. During the attempted assault, she thinks of herself as two separate people—one angry and terrified, the other calm and in control—and allows the second person to speak aloud, sometimes challenging and scorning Trenor and sometimes placating him. (This dichotomous self-image again dominates her thinking as she visits Selden to bid good-bye on the evening of her death and again shortly before death as she merges with the baby who has been named in her honor. It further confuses her understanding of herself because she has been trained to please men and people of higher status by chameleonlike behavior shifts. This double image appears frequently in Wharton's ghost stories, which she began to write about 1902.)

Traumatized after her escape, Lily rushes to her cousin, Gerty Farish, to avoid the isolation of her own room at her Aunt Julia's home and her aunt's questioning, but she is unable ever to tell even Gerty what caused her hysteria. She determines that she must "confess" to Selden the next day, because she expects him to meet her to declare his love for her. Instead, he never learns of her life-changing experience. By a tragic coincidence, he passed the darkened Trenor house at midnight and glimpsed Lily and Gus in the light of the doorway as she left. Falsely assuming that she has had a scandalous liaison, Selden the next day leaves for Europe in anger, does not see her for months, and never allows her to explain what he saw. That same day, Lily, already obsessed with paying whatever debt Trenor claims she owes, seeks a loan from her staid aunt, who is so shocked by Lily's appeal for money supposedly to pay gambling debts that she evicts her, cuts off her allowance, and virtually disinherits her.

In Book 2 Lily has accompanied some newly rich people, whom she advises on matters of social strategy, on a cruise aboard the yacht of Bertha Dorset, the jealous former mistress of Selden, who is now having an affair with Ned Silverton. To cover her own misbehavior, Bertha at Monte Carlo falsely accuses Lily in public of adultery with her husband, George Dorset. Selden is present but does not defend her. Lily's access to the rich and aristocratic society immediately disappears: she no longer is an asset to any hostess, and even speaking to her becomes a liability to her former associates. Shunned by her aristocratic relatives and by the haut monde, Lily is forced to seek solace and material support from still another group, the nouveau riche (the Brys, the Gormers, and Simon Rosedale).

In her struggle to survive, Lily even thinks of marriage to the vulgar millionaire Simon Rosedale, but though he pities her, offers her money, and gives her advice about fighting back by blackmailing Bertha with incriminating letters that prove Bertha's adultery with Selden, Rosedale makes clear that he cannot now profit from marriage to her. For a time, Lily earns her living as secretary to Norma Hatch, a divorcée of questionable repute, until Selden appears and disapproves. She then finds employment in a millinery workroom, but lacks the ability to do fancy sewing and the physical endurance to keep her job. Unemployed, malnourished, and suffering from insomnia, on the evening of her death Lily makes a last visit to Selden, who, despite his idealistic talk, reflects the obtuseness and caution of a society that overvalues conventions and appearances. At his home she reverses her decision to blackmail Bertha with the letters in her possession—her only means of regaining her acceptance in society. She rests in a park, and as it grows dark is given refuge in the slum kitchen of Nettie Struther, a poor working girl to whom she had once given money. Wharton emphasizes the "continuity of life" that Lily discovers in the dingy kitchen: holding Nettie's baby (who has been named in her honor) is now more important to her than Selden's lofty talk of a "republic of the spirit." Nettie and her husband accept each other for what they are. On this basis of mutual trust, they build a shelter for themselves and their child against the harsh world outside, though Lily sympathetically recognizes how tenuous even such a shelter may be: "it had the frail, audacious permanence of a bird's nest built on the edge of a cliff" (*HM*, 517).

Finally, in her room, Lily is exhausted, but victorious over her temptation to blackmail the enemy who has destroyed her reputation. Now she uses almost all of a small legacy that has just arrived from her aunt's estate to pay her other destroyer, Gus Trenor. It is a silent and lonely victory, and her heroism will never be recognized or praised. Having no money left for food or medicine, Lily in a confused condition takes an overdose of chloral even as she thinks of facing the next day. She dreams of the warmth of the baby next to her, of Nettie's wish that her child will grow up to be just like Lily, and of her affectionate farewell to Selden earlier that evening. She dies during the night, having achieved a selfless humanity.

Selden's arrival the next morning—too late to tell her he loves her—does not provide a sentimental ending to the novel. He may have been facing the possibility of proposing marriage, which he has been mulling somewhat fearfully for almost two years, but if he momentarily regrets having missed the right time for declaring his love, he moves about her room with little sign of grief. Seeing a little tray of beautiful, colored items (a rose-colored pincushion, some gold-capped bottles, some tortoiseshell hairpins, and a piece of lace), he does not treasure these as objects connected with Lily but shrinks from their "poignant intimacy." The rest of the room, with its shabby furnishings, reminds him not at all of Lily as the lover of beauty or of her discomfort in these surroundings. He quickly averts his eyes from the empty medicine bottle and glass. His strongest emotion comes from discovery of the envelope addressed to Trenor and he relives the shock he initially felt when he saw Lily leaving Trenor's house. Remembering the "bad Lily," he wonders whether she wrote the letter to Trenor before their visit the previous evening. Angrily, he thinks that his seeing this envelope has "unhallowed the memory of that last hour, made a mock of the word he had come to speak. . . . He felt himself flung back on all the ugly uncertainties from which he thought he had cast loose forever. After all, what did he know of her life?" (*HM*, 529). Upon seeing the check, he considers it merely as evidence of a disreputable relationship between Lily and Trenor.

This final irony reinforces the dominant sardonic tone of the novel.

Wharton's ironic view that moral integrity hampers rather than rewards a good person in this society does not waver. Lily remains a strong and admirable woman who is yet vulnerable to a materialistic and predatory society and to her own impulses and rootlessness, but she gains insight, compassion, and emotional depth from her disappointing and sometimes sordid experiences. Like Gerty Farish, she gains "that sharpening of the moral vision which makes all human suffering so near and insistent that the other aspects of life fade into remoteness" (HM, 243). She is a fragile "flower," but her fine instincts and her developing ability to see her society for its false values and its cruelty refine her sensibilities throughout the latter half of the novel. This society destroys her, but she is also superior to it.

Subordinate Themes and Characters

Besides Selden, the other most fully developed characters are Gerty Farish and Simon Rosedale. Though Lily is somewhat contemptuous of them, she turns to them at times of crisis. Gerty, a social worker of aristocratic family, is plain and allows herself to be taken for granted. She has much strength of character; but she is not idealized, nor is she presented as an angel of mercy. Even while Gerty selflessly comforts Lily, she struggles against her jealousy of Lily's beauty and popularity. Although Gerty's concern for others and her independence as a "new woman" are more laudable than Lily's weakness and parasitism, Wharton never lets Gerty upstage Lily. Lily has a magnetism and a sexual vitality that gain sympathy for her in a way that Gerty's dedication does not.

Simon Rosedale is a more complex character than some critics have judged him to be. According to Walter Rideout and Geoffrey Walton, he is a coarse and evil man designed to contrast with Selden and his fineness of spirit.[3] They therefore see as degradation Lily's eventual willingness to marry Rosedale in order to survive. Actually, anti-Semitism can account for much of Rosedale's social unacceptability. Even in the early part of the book, when Lily perhaps shares such prejudice, she also perceives certain formidable qualities in Rosedale. She recognizes an insecurity and ambition like her own in his attempt to be accepted in high society. She resents his awareness of her strategies, but she turns first to him rather than to Selden when her financial and social situation becomes desperate. Rosedale resembles Lily, as Elmer Moffat resembles Undine Spragg in The Custom of the Country. Both Moffat and Rosedale, who begin as totally negative figures, become candid appraisers of social hypocrisy who manage by their shrewdness to control, in part, the society that initially scorns them.

As Lily grows in perception through her suffering, her view of Rosedale alters. She detaches herself from the shallow standards by which he has been condemned, and she appreciates his clumsy concern for her illness, fatigue, and poverty. His urging her to blackmail Mrs. Dorset reveals his ability to fight an unscrupulous society on its own terms. By so doing, he teaches Lily its ruthlessness—something that Selden has never been capable of discerning. Rosedale is stronger than the "trivial society" because he judges it even while trying to invade it. The lethargic Selden, who thinks he rejects its values, is trapped by it from birth.

Looking back after thirty years at the writing of this novel, Edith Wharton recounted her struggle to fight off "subordinate themes . . . crowding to the front" and, along with them, characters irrelevant to her purpose, (*BG,* 207). She used some of these ideas and figures, however, to suggest the divergent aspects of New York society. Beyond the aristocrats, the moneyed established society, and the invaders, Wharton depicts the cheap restaurant patronized by secretaries and music students, the dingy boardinghouse, the scrubwoman supporting her invalid husband, the small factories that depend on the exploitation of labor, and the slums with their sickly inhabitants. In *The House of Mirth* Wharton documents changes in society at large as industrialism and financial speculation accelerate. She also documents the New York aristocracy's resistance to such change.

When Wharton explores subordinate themes and creates minor characters, she ordinarily does so only as they relate to Lily and her situation. She uses a unified point of view to the extent that, as Lily moves from the mansions and yachts of millionaires to the rooming houses of the slums, each level of society registers through her eyes. But each social group and Lily's experience with it filter through the eyes of at least one other person. This technique not only adds perspective to Lily's situation but also helps characterize the observers by contrasting their outlook and their behavior with those of Lily. Lily's point of view, though always dominant, is tempered by being held up against another's point of view.

Point-of-view characters are not similar to one another in this novel, as James would have insisted they be: They come from different classes and age groups. For Lily as the beautiful and impoverished aristocrat, the parties at Bellomont, the Trenors' estate, are exciting; for Selden as the languid young aristocrat, they are a waste; for Aunt Julia Peniston as the staid and elderly aristocrat, they lead girls toward immorality; for Nettie Struther as the young girl from the slums, they are balls attended by fairy princesses, which she enjoys vicariously in the newspaper accounts of them; and to Simon Rosedale as the vulgar millionaire, they are fortresses to assail. Lily looks condescendingly at Rosedale, but her view of him is not the same as that of others who snub him; and she eventually recognizes in him an opportunism akin to her own. Unlike Gerty Farish, Lily looks at the poor from a distance, even after she herself becomes poor. Selden apparently never sees the poor.

Another aspect of Wharton's mastery of her craft is the creation of minor characters with the greatest precision and economy—a technique she had already perfected in her short stories. Grace Stepney, for instance, registers immediately as a sharply defined individual when Wharton observes that she has a mind "like a kind of moral fly-paper, to which the buzzing items of gossip were drawn" (HM, 196). Though Mrs. Peniston is always in the background, she too is distinctly presented as Wharton defines her personality in terms of the objects she cherishes. Her furniture symbolizes her solid, old-fashioned stability, and it even persuades us of the reality of her shock when she hears the news of Lily's gambling debts. As she sits alone, convinced that Lily, her great-niece, has degraded her, her agitation seems to spread to the objects around her in the darkening parlor. She cannot fight immorality because it is as offensive to admit bad thoughts to her mind as to admit "a smell of cooking in the drawing-room" (HM, 204). She is as much a slave to propriety in her moral philosophy as she is in the circumstances of her daily experience.

Similarly, it is through physical objects (this time houses and property) that we see the Wellington Brys so precisely. Their ostentatious habits and their compulsive concern to rise in society are implicit in this one remark that describes their opulent mansion and its scarcely authentic furnishings: "One had to touch the marble columns to learn they were not of cardboard, to seat one's self in one of the damask-and-gold arm-chairs to be sure it was not painted against the wall" (HM, 212). Through minor characters, Edith Wharton reflects the amenities and the hollow pursuits of the rich at the same time that she reflects the viciousness of these people toward each other.

Because Wharton develops two main themes—Lily's destruction by her society and her victory over self-centered motives—she emphasizes not only the power that a materialistic culture exerts upon Lily, but also Lily's increasing insight, assurance, and sympathy for others. Though repeatedly a victim of circumstance, Lily must remain a free and unpredictable woman. An ambivalent individual, she acts freely and is also acted upon.

Although Wharton, in the main, clearly develops these principal themes, she sometimes obscures them by attributing Lily's tragedy to contradictory causes. At times, Wharton seems to endorse Lily's own view of her situation when Lily sees herself as the fated heroine of a Greek tragedy. At other times, she sees Lily's conflict in Judeo-Christian terms in which the individual's own character can become a battleground for the struggle between good and evil. At still other times, Lily is the protagonist of a naturalistic novel based on economic determinism in which forces of cosmic magnitude threaten to overpower her as she becomes the helpless victim of the hypocritical rich.

It is usually Wharton, as omniscient author, who expresses these principal interpretations of Lily's situation, but sometimes, far less appropriately, Lily and Selden voice them. Lily is, after all, a young woman who has lived for pleasure, who delights in society, who is seldom a speculative intellectual. It is doubtful, therefore, that she would speak with familiarity of the philosophical implications for her own situation of Greek tragedy. Wharton perhaps sensed this incongruity when Lily dramatizes herself as one pursued by the Furies after Trenor's attempt to rape her. She would hardly conceive her terror in precise literary terms. In order to make Lily's reference to the classics more credible, the narrator parenthetically remarks that Lily had once in a bored moment picked up a copy of Aeschylus that someone had left behind in a guest room. Nevertheless, Lily's impression of the Greek plays, we are to gather, is so powerful that at later times of crisis she cries out in horror at the Fates whom she imagines standing in the corners or pursuing her with clanging iron wings.

At other times of stress, Lily becomes acutely conscious of an almost schizophrenic split in her identity: forces of strength and weakness and of good and evil contend within her. As an Episcopalian, she is a nominal Christian, but she has never connected her own situation with Christian precepts. Part of the drama in the novel arises when she does so, suddenly and intensely. When she calls on Selden before her death, she had planned to carry through her project of blackmail and to relinquish her struggle against the evil in her own nature—to commit a kind of suicide of the moral self in order to survive in the physical and social world. But she discovers she cannot so separate the contrasting sides of her nature, and she throws Bertha Dorset's incriminating letters into the fire. As a human being, she must perpetually struggle to accommodate the good self and the bad self.

Wharton suggests that Lily's inherited tendencies and her early training make her helpless once she is thrust outside a parasitic existence in the houses of the rich. She is unable, as she finds out, to survive economically by her independent efforts as a wage earner. As a fixture in a hedonistic and fashionable society, she has become too specialized to do so, and she finally realizes, with some sense of despair, her limitations in adapting to change. When she is no longer in her niche, she is, as she explains in her farewell visit to Selden, a screw or cog that has fallen out of its machine. Even more strikingly, Wharton uses biological imagery to suggest Lily's final helplessness before cosmic forces: she is "an organism as helpless out of its narrow range as the sea-anemone torn from the rock" (*HM*, 486).

Lily is often not in command of her destiny; sometimes she is defeated by her emotions, her inclinations, and her personal weakness, sometimes by chance and impersonal social forces. Lily's behavior toward the millionaire Percy Gryce early in the novel provides an example of her drifting in accord with her impulses and shifting moods. Although she senses that he is ready to propose to her, as she had hoped, she breaks an appointment with him and goes for a walk with Selden because "the whole current of her mood" carries her toward him. Lily ought to assume more responsibility for such actions than she does, but Wharton prefers to interpret her indiscretion as a determinist might and to see Lily as "a waterplant in the flux of the tides." Ironically, however, her selfless acts, which are the result of moral choice, contribute as much to her destruction as does her irresponsible behavior. Selden, also a person slow to act responsibly and decisively, cannot rise above his excessive caution and his moods of the moment.

Despite the fact that the narrator implies Lily is finally defeated by weakness in the self caused by her early training and by the malignancy of an inflexible society, she does actually reveal a remarkable degree of versatility and adaptability. She simply does not possess these qualities in the degree necessary to survive in a ruthless society that entails for her changes too abrupt and too radical to cope with. Suggestions of her versatility abound. Posing in white draperies in the "tableaux vivants" at the Brys party, she delights Gerty and Selden as the Lily they know. But her unadorned figure startles others who cannot connect the image of simplicity she projects with the sophisticated Lily of their acquaintance. Gus Trenor, hypocritical in his lustfulness, complains that the white gown, which reveals the fluid lines of her figure, is in "damned bad taste," although it appeals to his sensual nature.

Lily seeks to appear under a different guise to each person who knows her, as if she were an actress with multiple roles in her repertoire to entertain a changing audience. She wants Selden to see her as a candidate for his vaguely conceived "republic of the spirit." Gerty Farish and Nettie Struther must see her as one who cares for the poor. She expects Percy Gryce to see her as a scholar who shares his interest in rare books and as a saint who walks demurely to church in a gray dress. Wharton describes Lily as "perfect" to each of her acquaintances; she is "subservient to Bertha's anxious predominance, goodnaturedly watchful of Dorset's moods, brightly companionable to Silverton and Dacey" (*HM*, 308). Selden, who observes her on a trip to Europe with the nouveau riche, perceptively recognizes that a hidden desperation prompts Lily to adapt, but chameleonlike, to the moods and impulses of her companions.

As a writer imbued with the ideology of Darwin and the naturalistic novelists, Wharton emphasizes Lily's defeat in terms of impersonal social and cosmic forces. The novel illustrates the power of society to destroy even those who, like Lily, possess character and tenacity. As Blake Nevius notes,[4] the cause of each of her downward movements in the social hierarchy is slight: the result is ironically disproportionate because impersonal factors determine so much of the outcome. Lily cannot evade the conventions that govern the exclusive and conservative society to which she belongs at first, nor can she evade the economic realities that govern the lives of the working class and affect women most harshly. Her inability to thrive without father, husband, or career education illustrates the limitation of choice for unmarried upper-class women, who were seldom prepared for a place in the competitive economy at the turn of the century.[5] For such women, to become "a moment's ornament" for a wealthy man might seem the most appropriate choice.[6] In her struggles Lily is defeated, in part, by a universe indifferent to the welfare of any individual or social group.

If Edith Wharton, as she herself recognized, learned much about her craft through writing *The House of Mirth,* she did not altogether master it in this novel. She overworks the element of ironic coincidence so that she can have Lily begin each stage of her life in a different social class, but she also reveals great skill in the composition of this book. She is expert in using contrasting scenes to balance one another, in coordinating simultaneous actions, in echoing late in the book earlier incidents, and in carefully modulating her dominant themes. In any case, Lily's struggle to survive, to find integrity, and to forgive her enemies lifts *The House of Mirth* beyond topical interest in an exclusive New York society of old aristocratic families and the nouveaux riche and makes it a novel of universal import and lasting appeal.

Chapter Three
Years of Turbulence and Growth: 1907–1912

After the *House of Mirth* appeared, Edith Wharton found that her "growing sense of mastery made the work more and more absorbing." Though friends now surrounded her in Paris and Lenox and though her affair with Fullerton had begun by 1907, she recalled that "the core of my life was under my own roof, among my books and my intimate friends. Above all it was in my work, which was growing and spreading" (*BG*, 293). In the next six years, despite the turbulence of her personal life resulting from the Fullerton affair and the end of her marriage, her vision expanded as she experimented with varied subjects and narrative patterns. In 1902 she had begun her experimentation with the ghost story, in which she covertly projected a curiosity and anxiety about the erotic. *The Fruit of the Tree* (1907) reflects her new interest in a fiction analyzing social problems, interpreting in a Freudian manner marital conflict, and experimenting with the use of ghost story devices in a realistic novel. *Madame de Treymes* (1907) and *The Reef* (1912) demonstrate her interest in adapting for her own purposes the techniques and themes used by Henry James.

The Fruit of the Tree

In *The Fruit of the Tree* Wharton is aware of social and moral problems akin to those undergirding the fiction of such contemporaries as Upton Sinclair and Jack London. Using as background a New England mill town, Hanaford, she raises the issues of factory safety, medical care for workers, the often unsavory relationship between factories and their insurance companies in the processing of workers' claims, the protection of female employees, day care for their children, the agonizing dilemmas posed by euthanasia, the prevalence of drug addiction, and the unregulated power of physicians over nurses.

Wharton analyzes the complexities of the two marriages of John Amherst at a time when not only single career women but many wives were struggling for equality and greater freedom and questioning male dominance in the family as well as in the business world. John Amherst, an engineer who is assistant manager of the Westmore Textile Mill, occasionally works in an equal and productive partnership with Justine Brent, a nurse, in their passionate pursuit of the safety and welfare of workers and their families. Amherst cannot in either of his marriages recognize the value of establishing equality between husband and wife. He believes unwaveringly in the working-class tradition that it is the man's responsibility and privilege to be the governor and protector of his family and to maintain its order and solidity. His determination to ignore the incipient shift in cultural attitudes toward power in marriage makes him value the companionship between himself and his first wife, Bessy Westmore, less than his friendship and idealistic reform efforts with Justine, particularly after Justine joins his household as companion and nurse to Bessy and his stepdaughter. When his first marriage fails after three years, he is philosophical and expresses some doubt about most marriages: "compromise is the law of married life."[1] Thereby he escapes his share of the responsibility for the failure of the marriage. His idealism where the welfare of his workers is concerned is so strong that to have compromised such commitment, as Bessy urges him to do in order to become more prosperous, would have constituted for Amherst a loss of honor. At the close of the book, his second marriage, to Justine, remains intact only through her efforts and her maternal dedication to her stepdaughter, Cecily Westmore. Justine, perhaps reflecting Wharton's own views, is cynical about the whole institution of marriage, even before she marries: "Most marriages are a patch-work of jarring tastes and ill-assorted ambitions—if here and there, for a moment, two colors blend, two textures are the same, so much the better for the pattern!" (*FT,* 369). Nevertheless, Justine tries to mediate a reconciliation between Bessy and Amherst. In doing so, she even counsels Bessy to be a "carpet" for him to walk over, if necessary. Such thinking prepares us for the submissiveness that becomes characteristic of Justine herself after she marries, although we have more often seen her in the earlier parts of the novel as the independent career woman. In any event, her attempts to help Bessy and Amherst repair their marriage make her own later accommodation to marital demands somewhat more credible and give the novel a continuity most critics have found lacking in its structure. Wharton suggests in this novel that even a well-intentioned man ought not expect his wife to worship him as a "lordly master," nor can he expect to maintain a harmonious relationship with two women at the same time, even when their differences appear to complement one another. It appears that Amherst can only be satisfied with a wife who would have all the best characteristics of both women. He needs both the beautiful and "chameleon-like" Bessy and the strength and social idealism of Justine.

Rather paradoxically, John Amherst, in spite of his conventional and conservative convictions, is one of the few strong, virile, and charitable men in Wharton's fiction. His blindness to the unhappiness he causes the two women he loves is reprehensible, yet his idealism is far stronger than that of Lawrence Selden, for instance, in *The House of Mirth*. His commitment to honesty in marriage is great, until near the end of the novel he misrepresents the dead Bessy's philanthropic plans as similar to his own. His battle against fraud and exploitation in industry is also genuine, and his advocacy of the interests of the working class is vigorous and tireless.

The Fruit of the Tree at first contrasts the two women: Justine Brent, the career woman, and Bessy Westmore, the beautiful, rich young widow and mother who has inherited the mill. When Amherst falls in love with Bessy, he is attracted by her doll-like, clinging, worshipful but petulant behavior and her extremely feminine appearance. In a conversation with his doting mother, he worries about his humbler working-class origins in the mill town. Shortly after the marriage, Bessy develops some independence and increasingly disobeys, usually covertly, the rules he insists upon for her welfare. Paradoxically, Bessy's quest for freedom brings her greater frustration than liberation. As a demanding, proud, and impulsive woman, she now meets defeat in all her confrontations with men. She has so long been the petted little girl that she accepts defeat in any fight, because she cannot withstand male disapproval—from her father, her lawyer, or Amherst. She never grows beyond her tendency to weep, scheme, and bargain, and she cannot be honest about her rebellious acts, because she fears critical response. Though she and Justine have attended the same convent school in Paris, before Justine's family lost its money and her parents died, only Justine has prepared herself for a career. Bessy is incapable of meaningful participation in decisions made by the board of her company, although she must vote as owner of the company. She is particularly susceptible to the domination of her father, who lives with her and John, who is involved in the governance of the mill, and who daily encourages the breakup of his daughter's marriage because Amherst urges Bessy to use her money and influence for the benefit of the workers rather than for increasing the profits of the corporation. Actually, Bessy disdains any woman who works for her livelihood, and she no more admires her friend Justine for pursuing her career as a nurse than Lily Bart in *The House of Mirth* admires Gerty Farish for becoming a social worker.

At first Bessy pleases her husband by coming from her Long Island home to take part in the Christmas festivities at the mill and even to tour the mill, but her determination to be free develops more perversely under the influence of her rich, pleasure-loving New York crowd. A gossip column reports that she has assisted her friend Blanche Carbury in arranging secret meetings with a married lover, Bowfort, at Bessy's home. Mrs. Carbury is supporting Bowfort with the money that she has recently obtained from her divorce settlement, and she has maintained her social status by quickly marrying a new husband, Fenton Carbury. This scandalous note shocks Amherst, and he forbids Bessy to entertain her divorced friend. He is also dismayed that Bessy's health seems threatened by her endless whirl of house parties so soon after she has lost an infant son, and he arranges for Justine to live with Bessy and her daughter, Cecily, as nurse and companion, since he must live mainly in Hanaford if his plans for reform at the mill are to progress. Justine continues to help Amherst in his plans for the health of the workers, and she becomes the trusted confidant of both Bessy and Amherst as their marriage conflicts grow. As in *The House of Mirth,* money and marriage cannot be separated. Amherst complains about Bessy's extravagant living, while she complains—as do her relatives and friends—that he uses too much of her fortune for projects that benefit laborers rather than management. She refuses to live in Hanaford, and he is angry that she later wants her money kept in an account separate from the funds for the mill, an account that only she will control. In her most dramatic gesture, she hires an architect to draw plans for a recreation center to be built near her Long Island home for the benefit of her fashionable friends. The project will take the funds Amherst had expected to use for a gymnasium and classroom building for mill employees and their families. Feeling only revulsion for Bessy after the stressful three years, he leaves to work in Argentina. Bessy in her final rebellion rides the spirited horse Impulse precisely because Amherst has forbidden her to ride it, fearing the possibility of a dangerous fall. She is thrown from the horse, and suffers a serious spinal injury. Amherst cannot be located. After Bessy endures days of severe pain, Justine mercifully gives her a fatal dose of morphine.

The last section of this very long novel, most critics have agreed, fails to develop organically from the first two-thirds of the novel in plot, character, and theme, although Wharton always insisted that the structure was its major strength.[2] Critics feel with justification that interest shifts too abruptly from the marital conflicts between Amherst and Bessy and the frustrated plans for reform of the mill's labor policies. Amherst has returned to the mill, and the point of view now shifts from him to Justine, his new wife. The competent, self-assured woman is at first joyful in their compatibility, but she diminishes in personal strength, courage, and even enthusiasm for her work as she pays blackmail money for a year to a drug-addicted physician, Dr. Wyant, in order to keep from Amherst the secret of her mercy killing of Bessy. When the blackmail becomes known to Amherst, the immediate cause of Bessy's death shocks him, but Justine's keeping a secret from her husband shocks him even more. In turn, his failure to understand her motivation and feelings as Bessy's friend and nurse disturbs her. She realizes that he fails to imagine the intensity of Bessy's pain and to recognize his own guilt in abandoning his wife when she thwarted his use of her money for his own goals. At this point, Justine suddenly realizes her situation has become similar to Bessy's. She also faces an inflexible husband who does not realize that honesty dies in a relationship when one spouse cannot communicate with the other because of fear.

Assuming that Amherst will welcome her absence, Justine takes a nursing position in another town. She reluctantly returns several months later, only because Amherst finds her and begs her to return. Her stepdaughter, Cecily, has been ill and needs her support. Even so, upon her return Justine must comply with the stringent irrational rules that bar her from working with him on projects at the mill and thus fully sharing his companionship. Before her marriage, she had been accepted and loved by him for her strength and decisiveness, but now these qualities in a wife dismay him.

After Justine's return, Amherst devotes his time obsessively to creating a Bessy who never existed—a suppliant saint, a woman whom he feels he now could love perfectly were she to appear again before him. Justine submissively accepts his behavior because she recognizes that guilt and remorse for his treatment of Bessy now motivate him. When he conducts a memorial service for Bessy before a crowd that includes applauding workers from the mill, he holds up blueprints supposedly for a workers' gymnasium that he says Bessy planned before her death. Justine is appalled at this dishonesty, because the blueprints are those drawn for a recreation center Bessy had selfishly planned for her fashionable New York friends. After the service, he is flushed with pleasure because he has elicited from the workers some of his own adulation for the new and lovable Bessy he is creating. Like some of the characters in Wharton's ghost stories, Justine now recognizes the powerful presence of an invisible dead rival in her marriage and thinks her husband is possessed by a spell of madness. Having pitied Bessy for two years because of her horrible injury, Justine now finds herself fighting against a hostile force, a formidable presence deriving strength from Amherst's early romantic illusions about Bessy. In her mind, she recalls the details of Bessy's selfishness, hostility, petulance, hypocrisy, and incapacity for full maternal love. Justine now reconciles herself to her marriage only because she wishes to be a better mother to Cecily than Bessy could have been.

Her decision to keep this flawed marriage intact is similar to Isabel Archer's decision to return to her husband at the close of Henry James's *Portrait of a Lady* in order to be near her stepdaughter and to support her. Here, as in Wharton's two preceding works, *The House of Mirth* and *Madame de Treymes,* a child influences a major decision of the heroine at the close of the book. Critics have tended to overlook Wharton's early interest in children and maternal love—particularly in childless women—though these critics recognize such interest in her later fiction. Justine's decision is not heroic, but it may be a wise compromise.

Her recognition of the ghostly former wife as her rival reflects Wharton's new interest, at this stage in her career, in the ghost story, particularly as she uses it to suggest the erotic. Later Wharton again uses the ghost of a now dead woman to explore the theme of the impossibility of a "double love," as in "Bewitched" and "Pomegranate Seed." In these tales, efforts by a male protagonist to support his present marriage while returning to a former lover who reappears as a ghost to seduce him result in his destruction. In *The Reef* Wharton subtly modifies this basic theme of the ghostly rival when Anna Leath finally refuses to risk sharing with another woman George Darrow's love for her after their projected marriage, just as earlier she had resented his violating their engagement by his brief affair with Sophy Viner. Darrow seeks to reassure Anna that his love for Sophy died early, but Anna remains haunted by the sense that the ghost of his affair will rise again—as it does in her own mind. Sophy, like a ghost, vanishes in the night, leaving a note saying she is fleeing from her own approaching marriage to Owen Leath in order to devote her love only to the phantom memory of her dead affair with Darrow. Later, in the close of *The Age of Innocence,* Wharton returns to the theme of the dubious nature of a double love and the seductive nature of a dead or invisible rival. In Paris, Newland Archer, many years after he relinquished his beloved Ellen Olenska, now chooses again to devote himself only to his wife, May—this time to her memory, for she has recently died—instead of trying to renew his passion for his former love.

In *The Fruit of the Tree* Wharton failed to encompass in a satisfying structure her disparate concerns—with social issues, marital conflict, and the possibility or impossibility of a double love. In this novel she does not fully master the requirements of elaborate plotting. Nevertheless, she does create three interesting characters and provides a searching analysis of the difficulties involved in building a good marriage, particularly at a time when the traditional roles of men and women in all phases of life were being revised.

Wharton's colorful and precise use of detail in *The Fruit of the Tree* reinforces the insights into her characters and their conflicts and more than adequately compensates for any structural shortcomings. Bessy, for instance, finds the mill town oppressive and the mansion she has inherited there cold and provincial. Numerous details reveal her unrest, sense of isolation, and disappointment. The chandelier in the red satin drawing room suggests to her a latent hostility in the atmosphere; lamps would have lent greater warmth and intimacy to the house. She also sees the town's lack of sophistication reflected in the decor of the room with its bronze Indians on velvet pedestals and its trite landscapes. When she inspects the factory, she hurriedly observes only those details distasteful to her—grease, dust, belts, and wheels—and fails to see the room and its dangerous machinery through the eyes either of a worker or a reformer.

Amherst, aware of the beautiful and rich young widow's limited vision, foolishly adjusts his own vision to Bessy's and sees familiar surroundings as she would see them and is accordingly ashamed of them. He fears the impression that his mother's modest house will make on her, and he recoils from "the week's wash flaunting itself indecently" and "the expected whiff of 'boiled dinner' " (*FT,* 69) Physical details also suggest Amherst's alienation from Bessy three years later, when the childlike Bessy has come to resent Amherst's preoccupation with reform, and when he in turn has come to resent her failure to share his aspirations. The frills of her boudoir, which once had enchanted him as extensions of her mystery and loveliness, are now distasteful. These adjuncts of femininity have become the measure of his disillusionment rather than symbolic of the ecstatic emotion he had formerly experienced with her.

With similar economy, Wharton characterizes her minor figures by mentioning only two or three details. Mrs. Truscomb's strength and vulgarity, her wealth and dubious pretentiousness, for instance, are suggested all in one phrase: "a large flushed woman in a soiled wrapper and diamond earrings" (*FT,* 29).

Madame de Treymes

In *Madame de Treymes,* a novella that appeared in the same year as *The Fruit of the Tree,* Wharton achieves a more unified effect. She places American characters against a European background, elaborates a single psychological conflict, observes detail minutely, uses dialogue that echoes natural patterns of speech, and gives unspoken soliloquies to her point-of-view character. These techniques suggest the Jamesian influence that was to become even more significant in her next works, *Ethan Frome* (1911) and *The Reef* (1912). Several themes underlie the action and unify this novella: the materialistic exploitation of the Americans by the French; the contrast between the beautiful upper-class French woman's sexual freedom, as exemplified in the behavior of Madame Christiane de Treymes, and the rigid control imposed upon her by patriarchal authority and Roman Catholicism; and the contrast between the freedom Durham and Fanny Malrive enjoy as American Protestants and the strict discipline imposed upon them by their own sense of responsibility toward each other and toward Fanny's child. Wharton's concentration on only three characters and her consistent use of Durham's point of view throughout this book add to its powerful unity.

In a slow beginning, three pages pass while in the elevator Fanny Malrive buttons the gloves she had carelessly forgotten to put on before leaving her home, an oversight "charged with significance to Durham," who hopes to marry her following her divorce from Madame de Treymes's brother. But Edith Wharton's characteristic concentration and economy immediately surface after Durham's opening reverie. In the Tuileries gardens the conversation of Durham and Fanny focuses on the pivotal forces in the plot: her resolve to keep her only son close to her maternal influence, her indefinable fear that her relationship with the boy may be threatened by her husband's family, and her hesitation to remarry because of this fear.

Because Fanny is apprehensive about the family's probable disapproval of the divorce and her remarriage, Durham elicits its support through an appeal to Madame de Treymes, Fanny's sister-in-law. She surprises him by agreeing immediately to plead his case, on condition that he pay the debts of her lover, who stands on the brink of disgrace. Shocked at her proposal, Durham refuses to associate Fanny's name with an unsavory situation, even to further his own happiness. To his further surprise, Madame de Treymes announces the next day that she has already persuaded the family to approve the divorce; and her only reward, she now says, will be in observing his happiness when he returns to marry Fanny. Later, Durham learns that Christiane's reward, ironically, will be her vengeful watching of his misery because the family approval of the divorce underlies a conspiracy to gain custody of the child should Fanny ever remarry. Christiane coolly advises Durham against enlightening Fanny about this plan. He can later comfort Fanny, Christiane believes, by fathering a son to replace the one whose custody she will have lost. Christiane seems bewildered that Durham will not marry Fanny at the price of such deception.

The presence and strength of Christiane de Treymes shift the focus of the book from Fanny's conflict to Durham's dilemma. Fanny never needs to decide between Durham and her son because Durham and Madame de Treymes work out her destiny for her, as though she were a symbol in an algebraic equation. Christiane professes love for Fanny and good will toward Durham; yet she is, in reality, self-centered and resentful of the restrictions imposed upon her by a society that will not permit her to divorce an incompatible husband. Both a magnetic and a sinister woman, Christiane is the moving force behind a social conspiracy and may later be its chief victim.

The Reef

Like classical drama, to which Henry James compared it, *The Reef* develops in five equal sections. Book 1 is confined to a few days in October, mostly spent at Givre, Anna Leath's château. The action begins swiftly, as one of Wharton's short stories might. During a spring rain on a Dover pier, the thirty-seven-year-old American diplomat Darrow casually meets Sophy Viner, a young girl who has just lost her situation with Mrs. Murrett, a rich American of doubtful reputation. Three months earlier, Darrow had felt his youthful love for the recently widowed Anna Leath revive. Angered by a telegram from Anna that casually tells him not to come, he crosses the Channel with Sophy; attends the theater with her; and invites the penniless and stranded woman to rest in the room adjoining his hotel suite. He tells himself that Sophy is a child for whom he is providing a holiday, but, in the last paragraph of Book 1, when she brings him a letter from Anna late at night, he drowsily kisses her and throws Anna's letter, unread, into the fire.

Tension increases as Darrow arrives some weeks later at Givre, where Anna has been struggling to attain family approval for the betrothal of her stepson, Owen Leath, to the new governess (for Anna's daughter). Madame Chantelle, Anna's mother-in-law, must approve the betrothal because Owen will inherit the family estate upon his marriage. The governess and intended bride, Darrow soon discovers, is none other than Sophy Viner. Though free in his own conduct, Darrow now is surprisingly conventional. Because of their affair in Paris, he does not respect her, and he suspects her of marrying Owen for his money. He cannot, of course, tell Anna the reasons for his disapproval of Owen's plans. Ironically, Sophy refuses, in Book 4, to discuss plans for her wedding with Owen and mysteriously asks to leave Givre, because she has discovered that she still loves Darrow and wishes to keep her memory of their affair intact.

Sophy is not the only sensitive, imaginative woman in the novel; Anna Leath also has a Jamesian sixth sense that enables her, like Maggie Verver in James's *The Golden Bowl,* to divine the previous intimacy of the man she loves with another woman. Accordingly, in Book 5, Anna also renounces her wedding plans. Wharton then traces Anna's intense inner conflict as she gradually tries to accept Darrow after she can no longer idealize him and as she learns in the process to accept her own passionate, though repressed, nature. Unfortunately, her growth has its limits because her tolerance has limits, and she never accepts Sophy as a human being of integrity, and she never fully trusts Darrow again.

Though presented as a woman of charm and grace, Anna remains a prisoner of the inhibitions, narcissism, and rigid mores inculcated by her Old New York upbringing. Like May Archer in *The Age of Innocence,* Anna is passionate, jealous, and possessive in her love; and, like May, she is both limited and protected by convention and by belief in monogamous marriage. Though controlled and outwardly passive, both refuse to accept infidelity and are stern about the banishing of a rival, even a woman previously seen favorably as a member of the family. If both appear to be old fashioned, both are ahead of their time in rejecting a double standard.

Through a flashback technique used at various points in the novel, Wharton economically reveals the origins of Anna's complex nature and of her present reactions to Sophy by showing Anna as she was before her first marriage. Interested even then in Darrow, she had tried to appear unemotional, though she had longed to kiss him; and she mistakenly thought that her lack of demonstrable ardor would awaken his passion. At this point, Darrow had felt attracted to her but not to the extent of being willing to surrender his bachelor freedom; and Anna had become intensely jealous of less inhibited and less proper women who win their men. When Anna Leath learns in Book 5 of Sophy's affair with Darrow, she experiences a resurgence of the frustrated desire and of the acute jealousy of "freer" women that she had felt some fifteen years earlier.

With Darrow's return to Givre, her awareness of sensation becomes abnormally keen as she feels her former passion for him gain ascendancy over her. In her marriage to Fraser Leath, a man of cool temperament, her emotions had found sublimation in affection for her little girl and for her stepson. Darrow notes with some satisfaction that while Anna indicates no regret for her choice of a quiet husband, who had painted watercolors and collected enameled snuff boxes, she speaks of him impersonally as if he were some historical figure of a character in a book she had read. In contrast, every detail that connects her with Darrow becomes for her sexually charged: she finds that his letters give a keener edge to her senses as she touches the paper; she hears not only the sound of his step but the echo of it; she hears his voice from a distance before anyone else does. As he approaches, she feels the plants that she arranges become suffused with vital energy: "Every sensation of touch and sight was thrice-alive in her. The gray-green fur of the geranium leaves caressed her fingers."[3] Even Darrow's coat and hat mingled with hers on a bench suggest to her exacerbated psyche "a sense of homely intimacy."

Wonder pervades her inner being at her present sensuous awakening, even though she is at the same time fearful of some of its implications. She is almost overwhelmed by the "distance" between what she is now and what she had only recently been. She feels some regret as she sees the shadows under her eyes and realizes that her youthfulness is passing. So strong is her love for Darrow, however, and so confident is she in the strength of his passion for her that she dismisses such passing moods of insecurity. No longer guarded in her attitude toward him, she becomes vulnerable to the shock of learning that he had recently taken Sophy as his mistress. She cannot believe that an experience in the past can be relegated to the past; for her, it must, of necessity, have repercussions in the present. She is irrationally torn between a desire to obliterate all thought of Sophy and an obsession to ferret out every detail of the relationship between her and Darrow. When Darrow makes light of the affair as only a moment's diversion, such an admission is for Anna only a sign of Darrow's callousness, insensitivity, and masculine complacency.

The psychic interplay between Anna and Darrow and Anna's anguished introspection after she divines the truth in Book 5 account in large part for the richness of the novel. Darrow at first recognizes that fear keeps Anna from facing reality, but he later reproaches her for not trying to understand his vulnerability to sexual attraction the previous spring. When she cries that she does not *want* to understand, he charges her with a failure of imagination and sympathy. She then assumes, in fact, that he regards her as emotionally cold.

At this point, he shifts abruptly and illogically from his halfhearted defense of Sophy's impulsive response to him, from his honest appraisal of his part in their affair, and from his resentful censure of Anna for her lack of understanding of passionate behavior. He begins what even he must recognize as a dishonest placating of Anna. He, like Anna, actually remains trapped in the conventional pattern of thinking that categorizes women as either "fallen" or "pure." Later, however, his pattern of persuasion again shifts when he admits to Anna that, while he took it lightly, Sophy saw their affair as no "slight and surface thing." He chides Anna for priding herself on her ignorance of all behavior between men and women that differs from her limited range of experience. He strives to force her to see that living involves compromise. Rather petulantly, Darrow contends that he has already expiated his error by suffering the humiliation of having to explain the old affair to his betrothed.

As Darrow's moods and arguments shift from moment to moment in his frustration, so also does Anna vacillate between renouncing and accepting Darrow. Finally, she accompanies him to Paris, with the wedding plans again scheduled. In the train compartment, however, her shyness overcomes her urge to express passion and tenderness, and she again becomes the inhibited Anna of her youth. She pretends to read so that she can maintain a proper dignity and distance and can avoid meeting his eyes; but a second later she resents his reading, as if it presages that he will soon take their love as a matter of course. Her desire for him is so great that she feels misery and dread, even when he leaves her for a moment to buy a newspaper. As he kisses her, leaning in through the window of her cab, she momentarily feels self-reproach at her triumph because she remembers the cry of Sophy Viner, who has lost him: "I knew all the while he didn't care."

Had the book ended here, the reader could satisfyingly identify with Anna Leath in her victory as she regains Darrow's love and her love for him and as she attains a momentary compassion for Sophy. But the last two short chapters undercut Anna's magnanimity and reveal her as all too human. Nevertheless, what she loses in spiritual stature she gains in credibility. She broods over the fact that Sophy, through her impulsive and total surrender to Darrow, found an emotional experience of an intensity that Anna, after her life of reserve, may never be able to emulate. Torn by jealousy, Anna now peremptorily demands that Darrow recount every detail of his liaison with Sophy. He recoils from Anna and refuses to satisfy her curiosity and unacknowledged demand for vicarious experience.

Anna is fascinating to analyze as she vacillates not only in her feelings for Darrow but also in her feelings toward Sophy—from jealousy, to revulsion, to curiosity, to sympathy, to magnanimity, and to dissimulation. The next morning she seeks Sophy at her sister's shabby hotel to tell her that she is relinquishing Darrow to her. This gesture is idle, for the sister announces that Sophy has just left for India with her former employer, Mrs. Murrett. Sophy's sister, a singer, is undoubtedly a courtesan, and she now foreshadows for Anna what Sophy may with the years become. The visit thus provides Anna with a rationale for disregarding Sophy as an individual and for rejecting her as one whose destiny will embrace easy living, luxury, and promiscuity. More important, it also forces Anna to reject Darrow, because he is untrustworthy, insensitive, and dishonest and because she needs security. Now, she cannot evade this conclusion by nobly relinquishing him to the younger Sophy.

In a letter dated 4 December 1912, Henry James enthusiastically praised *The Reef* for its psychological unity and intensity, and he admired the creation of Anna Leath as "an exquisite thing . . . a wonder of delicacy."[4] The reverberations of a single situation upon four characters, the psychological interplay between Anna Leath and George Darrow, the long unspoken soliloquies, the economical dialogue, and the delicate adjustment of Anna's idealized views to new emotional experience again reveal the influence of James. Yet the frequent alternating of point of view between Darrow and Anna seems to show that Wharton never rigidly followed the precepts of another author.

As in James's work, the turning points in the lives of the characters derive from an individual's sensitive reaction to scenes in which nothing seems to be happening. Owen Leath, for instance, suspects something amiss when, looking up at the library window, he observes Darrow who is having his first meeting alone with Sophy at Givre. Though Owen is beyond the range of hearing, he perceives their agitation because Darrow's head is buried in his hands and because Sophy stands looking fixedly away from him. Anna similarly reveals the same sharpened perception when she tests Owen's suspicion that Darrow and Sophy have previously known each other. After her casual mention of Owen's "foolish" notion to Darrow and Sophy, she expects them to look at each other in surprise. Instead, their studied avoidance of each other's gaze gives her a sure indication that they have been acquainted previously and have hidden this fact.

As in Wharton's earlier novels, background reinforces action and mood. Givre stands for the tradition that supports, as well as inhibits, Anna and for the loveliness, the dignity, and the orderliness that she seeks to maintain in her life and the lives of those around her. It contrasts with Darrow's unattractive hotel suite in Book 1,[5] with the lavish surroundings of the newly rich Americans in Europe, like Mrs. Murrett, and with the untidy room inhabited by Sophy's sister. The description of Fraser Leath's small library, where so many crucial conversations occur, emphasizes the stability he had provided for Anna before his death. Anna, in fact, needs for her fulfillment *both* the solidity of Fraser Leath and the "winds of passion" brought by Darrow, who, perhaps symbolically, plans to take her to South America to live. That her new love builds on the sure but static nature of her first marriage is communicated only by suggestion and never by direct statement. Anna Leath wants what Wharton had so recently in her poetry insisted that she too wanted— physical ecstasy and a lasting love that was a spiritual merging of the lovers. But Wharton could also identify herself with Sophy Viner as a woman taking risks and acting on instinct rather than reason in her passion for a man who, it appeared, did not intend to love only her or to love her for a lifetime. Anna's shiftings about in her decisions, her moods, her plans, her love, and her anger continue as her conflicts are still unresolved by her final decision to reject Darrow. Throughout the novel she acts not only from distrust and jealousy but also in line with positive values and principles related to her beliefs in monogamous marriage and fidelity. Darrow argues that she is sacrificing her life's happiness for an impossible ideal, and he does so in terms that Wharton herself had used in several earlier works. What she had called "the inutility of sacrifice" he calls "the monstrousness of useless sacrifice." He cannot recognize the validity of Anna's contention that it would be a greater sacrifice for her to be tied in marriage to a man she cannot trust. Darrow sees Anna as a woman "still afraid of life, of its ruthlessness, its danger and mystery," even after she has been able to acknowledge her passion for him. Certainly she seems to be in a different universe from Sophy's disreputable sister near the close of the book. But if Anna has been inhibited by her old New York upbringing, Darrow's understanding has been limited by his early acceptance of the double standard. Neither of them can change, and their struggle must remain unresolved.

The chief symbol, the reef, unifies the novel. A natural phenomenon that cannot be avoided, a danger that is ominous, a fate that destroys without warning and emanates from beneath an apparently tranquil sea, the reef has suddenly risen before all four characters. In the face of this threat, Anna struggles to retain a romantic idealism. She makes an agonizing sacrifice that she agrees will help no one else, and she arbitrarily refuses to make what Wharton had once called the "pitiful compromises" with fate that all people must make. Anna defends her behavior in rejecting Darrow by declaring to herself, as the narrator reports: "There *was* such love as she had dreamed, and she meant to go on believing in it, and cherishing the thought that she was worthy of it. What had happened to her was grotesque and mean and miserable; but she herself was none of those things, and never, never would make of herself the mock that fate had made of her" (*TR*, 302). Jean Gooder, like many others, concludes that Anna, in spite of her newly awakened sexual response, remains "locked into her own life" and cannot make "the leap of understanding that would have saved them." Most critics blame the bleak ending upon Anna's excessively rigid morality and unforgiving nature, and they identify Sophy as the more sympathetic character in the book. Moira Maynard is almost alone in writing an extended defense of Anna Leath, coupling it with a stern look at Sophy Viner and her thoughtless abandonment of Owen Leath, from whom Wharton inexplicably diverts our attention.[6] Although Wharton leaves many issues in this novel ambiguous, in order to emphasize the confusion and uncertainty of Anna Leath, George Darrow, and Sophy Viner, Maynard's decisive views force us to look again at the "common" interpretations of this novel, which is so rich in its nuances.

Because of its constricted scene and its intense psychological probings, *The Reef* contrasts greatly with *The Custom of the Country*, which Wharton began earlier but completed at about the same time. In *The Reef* Wharton sacrifices much of the dramatic power and the verisimilitude that might have resulted from placing the action in a more representative and more inclusive milieu. She did achieve a compression and a concentration that are impressive; and she also achieved the classical unities of time, place, and action at some cost but also with remarkable precision and dexterity.

Chapter Four

"Particular fine Asperity":
The Custom of the Country

The Reckless Picaro

The Custom of the Country (1913) is one of Wharton's indisputable master-pieces, and she always considered this novel among her greatest achieve-ments. The book has an imposing breadth and scope. The woman protagonist, Undine Spragg, moves with inexhaustible energy among people of several classes and cultures. The "custom of the country" that preoccupies Wharton in the novel measures the value of women—particularly beautiful women—in material terms, and is not confined solely to American culture.

Undine could not escape the implications of this "custom" even if she wanted to—just as Lily Bart, Bessy Westmore, Justine Brent, Sophy Viner, and Anna Leath in Wharton's earlier works could not. But Undine would not want to change the nature of an acquisitive society that encourages the viewing of human beings in terms of commodities. Her aim is not to escape but to exploit the "custom" for her own gratification and the enlargement of her sense of power. With her satiric eye, Wharton dramatizes impressively the clashes between individuals, classes, and cultures. Her sense of irony allows her to see most of her characters in a critical—sometimes comic—and not al-together unsympathetic light. If Undine's parents and Mrs. Heeney, the mas-seuse, are type characters, they also have compelling human traits. Though Wharton crowds the novel with characters, she incisively individualizes even her minor characters, making them memorable but not allowing them to di-vert attention from Undine or other major figures.

Although slightly shorter than *The Fruit of the Tree* and about the same length as *The House of Mirth, The Custom of the Country* impresses most readers as undoubtedly the most massive of Wharton's books, and it would be her greatest if she had conceived more of her characters with as much compassion as sardonic irony. The most commonly held critical objections to the book have always been the extreme nature of Undine's selfishness and pugnacity, her unlimited destructiveness—especially in the child cus-tody battle—and Wharton's use of caricature in her creation of this figure.

Even Warner Berthoff, who sees Wharton as undoubtedly "the most accomplished American novelist" of her generation, dismissed this novel as "a
broad satire of contemporary manners featuring, in gross caricature, the
social-climbing, man-eating Undine Spragg of Apex City. Sinclair Lewis's
dedication of *Babbitt* to Edith Wharton, a decade later, pays a just tribute
to this precedent. But the novel as a whole is put seriously out of joint by the
absoluteness of the author's hatred for her main character."[1] The most obvious response to this question of Wharton's hatred of the woman she created
as Undine lies in Wharton's greater hatred of what Undine so viciously
struggles with and takes advantage of—the custom of the country—a social repression that Wharton herself despised and possibly feared and that
she had allowed to devastate Lily Bart in *The House of Mirth*. R. W. B.
Lewis calls attention to a most interesting aspect of Wharton's attitude toward Undine when he comments on her use of her own experiences and
characteristics in creating Undine:

> Undine did, undoubtedly, stand for everything in the new American female that
> Edith despised. . . . There are smaller and larger telltale similarities. As a child
> Undine, like Edith, enjoyed dressing up in her mother's best finery and 'playing lady'
> before a mirror. Moffatt addresses her by Edith's youthful nickname, "Puss." Edith's
> long yearning for psychological freedom is queerly reflected in Undine's discovery
> that each of her marriages is no more than another mode of imprisonment; and
> Undine's creator allows more than a hint that the young woman is as much a victim
> as an aggressor amid the assorted snobberies, tedium, and fossilized rules of conduct
> of American and, even more, French high society.

Professor Lewis concludes that Undine is Wharton with all her "best and
most lovable" features cut away. He also sees in Wharton's personality the
characteristics of both Elmer Moffatt and Ralph Marvell.[2] A short time
before Wharton began planning this novel, two friends in the little circle
that gathered with Henry James and Wharton had written books presenting heroines somewhat like Undine, and Wharton had praised both
books—Robert Grant's *Unleavened Bread* (1900) and Howard Sturgis's
Belchamber (1903).[3] They may have influenced her drawing of the more
harshly conceived Undine.

Many critics have seen *The Custom of the Country* only as a satire of marriage and divorce conventions at the time of its writing, a satire both of the inflexible customs of the past and of the more permissive practices of the
present. Actually, Wharton explores all the commonly accepted conventions
and prejudices that contribute to the inequality of the sexes and she considers

their relationship to money and class. She views with sardonic insight the havoc caused by women who must fight these conventions in order to survive, but who may also enjoy doing so as they gain power by unscrupulous means. Seen as an analysis of the limitations imposed upon women and of their attempts to survive in an unequal world, this novel becomes Wharton's response to the questions she left unanswered in *The House of Mirth* and *The Fruit of the Tree,* and its implications remain as relevant today as they were when Wharton wrote these books.

Wharton's view of Undine is clearest as voiced by the detached social scientist Charles Bowen, who calls her "monstrously perfect," the woman who impresses by her beauty and intelligence but who has few scruples in pursuing her ends. In a culture that could have used her talents productively, her behavior might have been different, but Wharton also sees Undine as an unrestrained natural force that would have caused havoc in any patriarchal culture. Though she is a rebel, she is too individualistic to be a revolutionary or a feminist and not thoughtful enough to be a political radical. The ramifications of the novel are ambiguous: Is Undine naturally deficient in human feeling, or has human feeling in her been extinguished by "the custom of the country"?

In spite of negative response to the extreme destructiveness of Undine, many critics greeted *The Custom of the Country* as the important book that it is. Henry James praised it highly, as he had *Ethan Frome* and *The Reef,* which immediately preceded it. He liked her hard intellectual touch and her "particular fine asperity." Her prose, he thought, was "almost scientifically satiric."[4] This novel, along with *The House of Mirth, The Fruit of the Tree, Ethan Frome,* and *The Reef,* assured Wharton's lasting fame as a novelist and solidified her reputation among readers and critics alike.

Interesting parallels and contrasts emerge in the comparison of this novel with *The House of Mirth.* Although Wharton had written *The House of Mirth* in six months, she needed more than five years to write *The Custom of the Country.* In both novels she analyzed turn-of-the-century polite life, but, because *The Custom of the Country* covers a decade and because its completion was postponed, she was also able to extend her coverage to include a time when society had become more fluid. By the time of the later chapters the newly rich exert greater power, the aristocrats have grown weaker, and divorce, regarded as disgraceful in the early chapters, is soon commonly to be condoned. Whereas Wharton's compassionate treatment of Lily Bart tempered her satire in the earlier book, her detached presentation of Undine, an egocentric woman who flamboyantly pursues her shifting ambitions, imposes a distance between the reader and Undine that precludes sympathetic identification with her. In contrast to Lily Bart's destruction by a shallow society, Undine's imperturbable victory over it establishes the principal theme. She moves through a series of adventures with, as Blake Nevius suggests, the daring and recklessness of a picaro.[5] She never suffers defeat, only the frustrating discovery that whatever she gains is less satisfying to her after she has it in her grasp. She marries Ralph Marvell because he is a descendant of the exclusive Dagonets, who are "sweller than anybody." But, for one with her predilections, the subtleties of the aristocratic code and its humane if constricted values mean little when she learns that Peter Van Degen and his fellow Invaders (the newly rich) are "sweller" than the Dagonets. When she discovers that they have yachts and more money, she is insatiable in cultivating them. But things do not always go her way, for after she divorces Marvell to marry Van Degen, he throws her over. Consequently, she more deliberately engineers her entrapment of Raymond de Chelles, a French nobleman.

But in a sense she overreaches herself in this relationship also; to her chagrin, she discovers after marriage that the European aristocracy inhibits her more than did the New York aristocracy. Frenchmen of noble family, in the custom of a different but withal materialistic country, control their women rigorously, regarding their wives as bearers of sons and as decorative chattels to enhance their own social standing. In Raymond's ancient château in Burgundy, Undine must conform to the stultifying habits of his female relatives, who sit dutifully in the courtyard or in the cold halls and work for hours on their exquisite needlework in apathetic silence and who yield all respect to the old marquise and all humility to the men in the family. Because of such a placid life, no channel seemingly exists into which Undine can direct her own boundless, vital energy.

Undine is nothing if not self-willed, strong in the pursuit of power and relentless in her driving ambition. Since the de Chelles family interferes with her prerogatives as she sees them, she has no scruples in abandoning her second husband. She eventually divorces de Chelles to remarry Elmer Moffatt, now a millionaire. The reader gradually learns that Undine and Moffatt had eloped in Apex, Nebraska, but her parents had had the marriage annulled because they thought that he was not good enough for her. If Undine had sought her opposite in Ralph Marvell and Raymond de Chelles, she finds her own kind in Moffatt, who also sees in her a kindred spirit, though he is less deceitful. She is still insatiable for high status; and, even after this marriage, she thinks momentarily near the end of the novel of divorcing Moffatt to become the wife of an ambassador, until she discovers that divorcées are ineligible for such glory. Undine always wins over the circumstances of the moment, but winning, ironically, is never enough.

The fullness in *The Custom of the Country* markedly contrasts with the studied unity and focus Wharton had so recently attained in *The Reef*. In that novel almost no minor figures are present, and the action, after the prelude, is limited to a few days at Givre. Yet Wharton manages, surprisingly, to control the burgeoning energy and size of *The Custom of the Country* with a structure not unlike the one she employed in writing *The Reef:* she again divides her novel into five books and again imparts a sense of the movement characteristic of a five-act drama. Within each of the five sections, individual scenes clearly relate to one another and to an emerging pattern within that section. A single geographical setting and one set of related problems dominate each book and distinguish it from the others. Minor characters establish connections among the books, and so do the flashbacks into a past more remote than the earliest events in the novel.

Book 1 reviews the lives of the Spraggs in Apex, their fear of Moffatt, and their two years in New York. Book 1 closes with Undine's impending marriage to Ralph Marvell; most of the minor New York and Midwest characters appear and require little elaboration as they weave in and out of the later action. Book 2 spans the four years between Undine's disappointment with the European honeymoon and her decision to choose Peter Van Degen instead of Raymond de Chelles as a successor to Ralph; but she loves none of the three. Inconveniently for her ambitions and selfish designs, Ralph becomes critically ill; the family summons her, but she goes ahead with her plans to travel to Italy with Van Degen. Van Degen's later discovery that she did not rush to her husband when he needed her makes him decide against marrying her.

Two and a half years elapse between chapters 13 and 14 of Book 2, between Undine's discovery of her pregnancy and the day she misses the celebration of Paul's second birthday. Books 3 and 4 extend over the two years between her divorce from Ralph and her marriage to Raymond de Chelles. In Book 3, she adjusts to Van Degen's failure to claim her in Reno and launches her successful campaign to become the Marchioness de Chelles. In the shorter Book 4, Wharton focuses solely on Ralph's vain efforts to raise money in order to retain custody of Paul by bribing the avaricious Undine, who needs the money to attain an annulment from the Vatican so that she may marry de Chelles. Book 4 ends with Marvell's pathetic suicide, a symbolic event denoting the weakness of his class despite the fine moral qualities that Wharton has established for him. In Book 5, Undine grows disillusioned with her marriage to Raymond de Chelles, and she has no scruples about divorcing him and returning to her "soul-mate," Elmer Moffatt, who can at least offer her excitement, security, and power.

Undine as "the monstrously perfect result of the system"

"The custom of the country" denotes the prevalent worship of wealth and
the power it signifies, a power that can reduce human beings to things and
that measures them solely in material terms. American mores encouraged
men to value women as possessions and to provide them with the resources
for prestige and pleasure in return for their complaisance, companionship,
and sexual intimacy. This custom led to Lily Bart's helplessness in adversity;
Undine Spragg, on the other hand, exploits these materialistic values to her
advantage in her relationships with her father, her lover, and her three husbands. She succeeds in furthering most of her selfish designs in a world that
extols virtue and purity but actually rewards beauty and shrewdness. Lily
gradually becomes a complex human being; Undine, though more than a
caricature, remains less than fully rounded. She is a powerful symbol of physical attractiveness and money used in the service of an insatiable ambition,
and she seems less to fight against the inflexible moral standards and conventions than to be unaware of them. Taking for granted that, as a beautiful
woman, she can imperiously direct others and thereby achieve her purposes,
she sincerely desires the well-being of all those about her, provided they fall in
with her own expressed or implied wishes: "If only everyone would be as she
wished she would never be unreasonable."[6]

Undine does not develop as a result of her widening experience; she becomes, in fact, more compulsive in her self-centered activities. She views each
adventure separately and not philosophically. Wharton's own satiric vision,
however, broadens with Undine's successive experiences because they illuminate the weaknesses of each of the groups with whom she identifies during
the course of the novel: the New York aristocracy, the established first-
generation rich, the provincial French nobility, and the nouveau riche recently
arrived from the Midwest.

Scene is diversified in order to extend the reaches of the novel. In New
York it shifts from fashionable Fifth Avenue to the unfashionable Stentorian
Hotel to the Wall Street offices of Spragg or Moffatt. Beyond New York, the
characters move from Apex to Opake, Nebraska; to Skog Harbor, Maine; to
Reno. Undine spends her honeymoon in Italy, Switzerland, and Paris. Between marriages, she makes two journeys from France to New York. Married
to de Chelles, she divides her time between the Burgundian château and the
ancient family house in Paris. Her enjoyment of the Nouveau Luxe, where
rich and vulgar Americans gather, contrasts with the enforced frugalities
practiced at the Hôtel de Chelles. In addition to the shifting milieu, a pleth-
ora of minor characters of several nationalities and classes, most of them pos-

sessing individualized characteristics, give *The Custom of the Country* its amplitude. These characters add depth and perspective to Undine's activities and offer some continuity to her migrations. The book covers a decade, and successive references to the age of Undine's son establish the passage of time.

Flashbacks may occur in any of the five books. For instance, Undine never returns to Apex, but Wharton sketches her life in Apex and Elmer Moffatt's background there through the recollections, which appear at various points in the novel, of Mr. and Mrs. Spragg, Undine, and Elmer. Frequent references to the Spraggs's fashionably rustic summers in Skog Harbor and Lake Potash extend the canvas of the novel and introduce, with considerable economy, Undine's confidante and adviser, Madame de Trezak.

In addition to this retrospective technique, Wharton makes significant use of another technique of the dramatist—the choric figure who adumbrates, reflects upon, or interprets important events. Mme de Trezak is such a figure, but more important are Mrs. Heeny and Charles Bowen. Mrs. Heeny, a masseuse for society people, predicts Undine's future in the opening scene with her advice, "Go steady, Undine, and you'll get anywheres."[7] Apparently classless, Mrs. Heeny claims to know "everybody" and looks impartially, but sympathetically, upon people in all classes. She cheers up Mrs. Spragg, explains to Undine the intricacies of invitations and of replies to them, carries in her bag clippings from the society columns that keep Undine informed about the activities of her peers and rivals, and provides Undine with cautionary advice about, or encouragement of, her enterprises.

Charles Bowen, an anthropologist, observes life with the detachment of a scientist and only occasionally generalizes about his reactions. At one point, for example, he concludes that most men become slaves to the marketplace in order to give money and social power to their wives; but the men feel too superior to the women to discuss their work with them. Ralph Marvell, he stresses, is an exception to the system; he prefers a leisured, genteel existence and a sharing of his inner life with his wife. Marvell is not likely, in Bowen's view, to survive in a shifting cultural scene in which qualities more vigorous than Marvell's will be at a premium. On the other hand, he regards Undine as "the monstrously perfect result of the system" that has tended to discount, in the worship of Mammon and the pursuit of power, the qualities of integrity and of consideration for others that Ralph symbolizes. It is Bowen who brings together two cultures, each motivated by a different kind of materialism, when he introduces Raymond de Chelles to Undine. In so doing, he is something like the scientist who confines two incompatible kinds of animals in a cage in order to watch their adaptations to their environment and to each other.

Some critics have regarded Undine's unscrupulousness as evidence that midwesterners had brought with them to New York the excessive materialism, the disregard for morality, and the deterioration of culture that Wharton thought dominated modern life. Such a critical view inadequately apprehends her satiric range; for she felt, to some extent, that the hypocritical Dagonets of this world were more vulnerable to close scrutiny than were the more open and forthright, though admittedly philistine, midwesterners. Similarly, Undine's frank acknowledgment of her financial needs and her direct approach to economic facts contrast favorably with Raymond de Chelles's pretenses, his unwillingness to recognize his poverty, and his resentment of the rich Americans with whom he associates.

Clare Van Degen's refusal to divorce her unfaithful husband and openly to acknowledge her love for Ralph Marvell springs from moral cowardice, from her conviction that divorce is "a vulgar and unnecessary way of taking the public into one's confidence" (*CC,* 322). Mr. Spragg honestly states the principle that almost all the other characters live by: "I guess it's up to both parties to take care of their own skins" (*CC,* 261). But only he recognizes that Undine must return the pearls she accepted from Van Degen. Plump and ridiculous, Mrs. Spragg appeals to one's sympathies because of her "stores of lymphatic patience." Princess Estradina's promiscuity shocks even Undine, despite her awe of royalty. The inescapable fact remains that Wharton satirizes dehumanizing materialism and rampant egotism in whatever social classes in America or abroad these attributes are dominant.

Undine's Vanity: The Need for "a reflecting surface"

Though self-assured, Undine is, paradoxically, dependent upon others to help her decide what she wants. She identifies closely with the values of whatever group claims her attention, and she assimilates these values in her compulsive desire to dominate the group. In so doing, she illuminates the weaknesses of each group as she mirrors them. Her personality is a kind of tabula rasa as she absorbs each time into her own being the prevailing attitudes of those whom she confronts, while she eliminates from her mind the ideas and predilections that had been there previously. She also studies the responses of other people to her actions, waiting for their remarks or changes in facial expression. In this sense they serve as a mirror to her. There are narcissistic elements in her personality that obtrude when she regards herself in a mirror and rehearses her behavior.

It is no accident that the central image in the book is the mirror. As a child, Undine did not jump rope or play ball; instead, she played lady in front of a mirror. As she prepares for her first New York party, she enacts a pantomime before a mirror. Ralph Marvell's disillusionment on their honeymoon begins with his recognition that she does not want to be alone with him because she needs admiring crowds to provide a "reflecting surface" for her charm. Mr. Popple, the artist who paints society women, through his idealized, impressionistic portrait of her offers her another flattering mirror of herself. When Undine changes her life-style by changing her friends and husbands, she does so in order to find more significant mirrors for her beauty and untried ranges of behavior to copy. When she hears that aristocrats consider art to be important, she immediately visits a gallery. She follows a woman in furs, adapting her own facial expression and gestures to hers as she examines each work and makes notes in her guidebook. Only as Undine observes the reactions of others to each of her dramatic actions does she decide whether she has been really victorious or whether she should seek a different prize: "To know that others were indifferent to what she had thought important was to cheapen all present pleasure and turn the whole force of her desires in a new direction" (*CC*, 286).

The Custom of the Country encompasses the tragedy of Ralph Marvell's suicide and communicates the poignant loneliness of Undine's son. Nevertheless, the novel remains a comedy of manners that has the tone of a satiric fable. Geoffrey Walton compares the stylized comedy of this novel, with its vigorous caricatures and brilliantly visualized episodes, to Jonsonian drama.[8] As in Ben Jonson's plays, unusual names typify the sardonic surface of Wharton's satire. Undine was named for the successful hair tonic that transformed her father from an Apex druggist to a millionaire. Wharton makes one reference to the wavelike suggestion in the name in describing Undine's graceful figure and fluid movements, but she does not connect her with the myth of the undines (water sprites who gain a soul if they marry a mortal and bear a child) except by implication—Undine is incapable of gaining a soul and feels no love for her child. Undine's friends bear caricaturelike names: Mabel Lipscomb, Indiana Frusk, Maynard Binch, Lootie Arlington, Roviano, Madame Adelschein, Nettie Wincher, Ora Prance Chettle, Miss Stager, Claud Walsingham Popple, and Bertha Shallum. They come from such satirically envisioned places as Phalanx, Georgia; Opake, Nebraska; or Deposit, Kansas.

But Wharton's satire encompasses aristocrats as well as Invaders. She treats Marvell's suffering sympathetically when Undine claims Paul, but she is critical of his earlier embarrassment over the sensational press reports of the divorce. She implies that pride causes his irritation at such invasion of his privacy as an aristocrat for the pleasure of the common reader. He simply does not have the strength to ignore scandal or to take it in his stride even though he is innocent of the charges leveled against him. Particularly annoying to him is the repeated report that the divorce arose because of his single-minded devotion to business, since he has been unusually attentive to his wife and has entered aggressively into real estate promotion solely because of her insatiable demand for money. As a man lacking some ultimate degree of self-sufficiency, he is in the end more concerned with his reputation in the larger world than with proclaiming the truth about his situation. Wharton also exposes the failings of the French nobility, notably the men's arrogance toward women and the women's willingness to efface their individuality at the family's behest. Though Raymond de Chelles would not acknowledge the truth of the judgment, his behavior more often suggests inflexibility and hauteur than incorruptibility or regard for a living culture.

In praising the consistency of tone in this satirical comedy, we must except the presentation of Ralph Marvell. Wharton has presented his suicide and its attendant circumstances with such intensity that the sequences involving him depart from her characteristic impersonal mode in this novel. On the other hand, she establishes in convincing detail his frustrated aspirations, his disillusionment with Undine, and his possessiveness in regard to Paul—aspects of the book that communicate the inevitability of his despair. Through Ralph's eyes, as he gradually learns to see his wife as she is, Undine develops into more than a stereotype.

Though the inflexibility and the timidity of his class amuse Ralph, he loves and respects the old traditions, aristocratic decor, and conservative people, and he resents the newly rich with their vulgar ways more than he knows. In spite of his generosity and magnanimity, he has little power of self-criticism. He completely misinterprets, for example, his initial relationship to Undine: He sees himself as saving her from the influence of other Invaders by enlarging her vision, whereas it is he finally who adapts to her constricted standards and recognizes in himself, in at least latent form, those qualities that he most hates in her. For instance, when he criticizes her harshly for refusing to see in her pregnancy anything besides illness, anxiety, and expense, he suddenly realizes that he has himself been harboring a similar reaction to it. Again, after appealing in vain to her to curb her profligate spending, he recognizes that she is fundamentally more shrewd about money matters than he is and that he resents her determined bargaining.

As Ralph gets to know Undine better, he moves from worship to disillusionment to forgiveness to anger and finally to despair; but he never learns to meet her on her own terms or to struggle as determinedly as she does. He despises his own inadequacy without being able to do anything about it, and he realizes with despair that his education, training, and the very traditions that have molded him prevent him from decisively confronting the relentless Invaders who have taken Paul from him, as if the child were simply a possession to be bargained for. Undine's demand for custody of their son, simply to blackmail Ralph into paying her more money, exemplifies her cruelty and toughness.

Marvell's suffering invests the novel with depth and complexity, and his suicide adds to its human dimensions in its spectacle of a worthy man brought low by unforeseen, harsh, and inevitable forces. His death brings into focus the full degree of Undine's hardness and incorrigibility because she feels no remorse for the man whose death she has caused. His death is opportune because it allows her to marry a Catholic as a widow rather than as a divorcée and to become wealthier through her child's inheritance. She has a vague feeling of regret, however, about the sudden solution to her problems: "She continued to wish that she could have got what she wanted without having had to pay that particular price for it" (*CC*, 487).

As in earlier novels, Wharton here uses interior decoration, paintings, books, and furnishings to establish tone and to provide insight into her characters. For instance, the Spragg suite at the Hotel Stentorian exemplifies the tastelessness and extravagance of the newly rich, but Mrs. Spragg's discomfort, as she sits like a mannequin in the midst of her lavish furnishings, indicates that she is isolated and that New Yorkers have not accepted her even with her wealth. The Spragg's pretentious yet ugly possessions formed no part of their lives in the Midwest and are no valid mirror now of their lack of taste. The newly rich simply spend lavishly, and they distrust the apparent miserliness of those who have money and do not spend it. Undine thinks it strange that the Marvells have an old-fashioned wood fire when they could afford a clean and efficient gas log or polished electric grate. Her mother suspects that the Marvells were "trying to scrimp on the ring" because Ralph presents Undine with an heirloom rather than a new ring when they become engaged. The Spraggs and Moffatt are at least generous with what they have in contrast to the Marvells, Dagonets, and de Chelles who tend to feel that elegant manners compensate for their more furtive materialism.

Though Elmer Moffatt becomes a collector of paintings and books, these treasures, Wharton makes clear, do not reflect his taste so much as his eagerness to purchase them before other millionaires do. Even the nine-year-old Paul has more sensitivity than do his mother and latest stepfather. He senses that the tapestries they have bought from Raymond de Chelles belong in the drafty hall of the château, not in the Moffatt mansion, and he cries bitterly as if sensing his own isolation. He is alienated from the opulence that surrounds him, as was Mrs. Spragg ten years before. The child wanders through the mansion, and, reaching out for the beautifully bound books, finds that they are always locked up because they are too valuable to be read.

Wharton sketches in her minor characters so economically that they remain vivid whenever they appear at intervals in this long narrative. Clare Dagonet's hypocrisy is, for example, forcefully established from the beginning. She feels that she has demeaned her class by marrying a Van Degen from among the nouveau riche, but Wharton lets us know that Clare "repents" while wearing the Van Degen diamonds. Clare is able to condone Van Degen's infidelity simply because he makes life easy for her. Similarly, Wharton establishes the hypocrisy of Mrs. Marvell, who cannot see sexual matters clearly because she has been taught to evade such realities and is benumbed by fear of scandal. She registers shock when Undine tells her that Mabel Lipscomb may get a divorce simply to better herself socially. Yet Mrs. Marvell does not really consider the people involved in a marriage or its dissolution and is content to think of a divorcée as being in the category of the unmentionable: in New York "a divorced woman is still—thank heaven!—at a decided disadvantage" (CC, 95). In a character like Bertha Shallum, Wharton stresses the lack of inhibition that Undine sees as admirable and Raymond de Chelles rejects as vulgar. As she prepares for a day of pleasure with Undine, Bertha begins "screaming bilingually" at successive windows in the building's long facade.

In *The Custom of the Country*, Wharton conveys a sense of depth and abundance; and she reveals a sophisticated artistry and breadth of social knowledge. The most truly panoramic of her books, it is a stirring recreation of the pre-World War I milieu in America and France. Her sense of human values is strong, if somewhat deflected by her satiric impulses; and her insight into human motivation and her sense of the moral implications of her characters' decisions are firm and commanding.

Chapter Five

"Evasive Idealism" and the "Hieroglyphic World": *The Age of Innocence*

Stability and Change: The Novel's Significance and Structure

The Age of Innocence is, Edith Wharton's masterpiece. The work of a mature artist, it represents her in a more mellow and elegiac mood than that expressed in *The House of Mirth* or in *The Custom of the Country* in which the analytical impulse had dominated. Now the element of affection for a bygone age tempers her satire; and, if her criticism of the unworldliness of her aristocrats is still sharp, she sees that they also exemplified certain humane values by which they ordered their lives. For several years Wharton had been diverted from the writing of long novels and had published only shorter fiction, as if to acknowledge that the strain of creating a large-scale work was too great when the world was convulsed by war and by the sufferings that were its aftermath. Yet with *The Age of Innocence* she again produced a major novel that has challenged the attention ever since of readers and critics.

She controlled and articulated the action in this novel as perfectly as she had in *The House of Mirth,* though more subtly. Every incident and almost every remark, no matter how trivial, contribute to the central dilemma that faces Newland Archer in the book—the choice he must make between May Welland and Ellen Olenska, a choice he later realizes has been made for him by the society in which he grew up and by the two women who love him. The novel consists of two books of equal length; the first one moves from the engagement of Newland Archer and May Welland in January to their marriage in April; the second recounts the first eight or nine months of their marriage, and a very brief epilogue follows.

The tension in both books arises from Archer's love for May's cousin, Ellen Olenska, who has recently arrived from Europe after fleeing her husband, an abusive, dissolute nobleman. More concerned for the family's reputation than for Ellen's welfare, Archer joins her aristocratic relatives in persuading her not to seek a divorce lest she bring a breath of scandal upon them all. But, in a reversal of his prior arguments, he asks her (at the end of Book 1) to free herself and to marry him. Ironically, his earlier advice has been so effective that she now refuses happiness at the expense of others, particularly of May. One moment of expressed love accentuates in its intensity and poetry the suffering implied for both in Ellen's renunciation: "He had her in his arms, her face like a wet flower at his lips, and all their vain terrors shrivelling up like ghosts at sunrise".[1]

Book 2 begins with the April wedding and ends the following winter when Ellen Olenska returns to Europe, though not to her husband. On the eve of Ellen's departure, May stages a farewell dinner, an event that underlines the finality of Ellen's decision to leave. Her entire "tribe" of relatives and the luminaries of society who witness this solemn ceremony thus place an irrevocable seal on her plans. Ironically, most of them think that Ellen has been Archer's mistress; but they do not admit their suspicions in anything they say or do. In their eyes, Archer and Ellen get no credit for the rectitude that has been so difficult for them to maintain.

Later, when alone with Archer, May meets his announcement that he wants to go far away with her own announcement—that she is pregnant. The implacability of fate toward him strikes him with numbness. Romantic affection for May and his acceptance of old New York rules of respectability have trapped him, he sees with agony; and he further realizes that his own tendency to idealize women has also betrayed him. For one so constituted, it is impossible to disregard the expectations of his society that he will now do his duty toward her. The sparseness of the words that he can speak in this scene at the close of Book 2 suggests the shock that this final frustration engenders: "He looked up at her with a sick stare, and she sank down, all dew and roses" (*AI*, 342). With a cold hand, feeling only his own disappointment, he strokes her hair as he goes through the tender but now empty rituals of a husband and protector.

Ostensibly the novel should end here. But the single remaining chapter is integral to the total aesthetic structure of the novel. Twenty-five years elapse between Archer's perfunctory embrace of May and the final chapter. She has meanwhile borne three children and died after twenty-five years of marriage in which she was "generous, faithful, unwearied." For his part, Newland has been a "good citizen." Though he acknowledges to himself that he has missed the "flower of life," he also, like Wharton herself, realizes that this flower is as remote from most people as a lottery prize. With serenity he can now recall Ellen and his transcendent passion for her. He thinks of her not so much as an actual woman but as a figure from a book or as a woman in a picture. Finally, he also recognizes that May knew all along of his love for Ellen; and he now finds comfort in knowing that someone had guessed his secret and pitied him: "that it should have been his wife moved him indescribably." He sits for a long time across the street from Ellen Olenska's apartment building in Paris. Ultimately, he decides not to cross the street and sends his oldest son to see Ellen in his place.

If mellowness and tolerance are present more by implication in Wharton's earliest fiction, they now dominate her vision, and an assuredness and authority dominate her craft. *The Age of Innocence* is her most consistently articulated and sophisticated novel—one more perfectly wrought, through her control of subject, than her other two greatest novels. *The House of Mirth* and *The Custom of the Country* had tended at times to be too inclusive in scope or too encyclopedic in coverage, and she had not always been able to achieve a form that could contain the abundance of her inspiration.

When she attained classic form in *The Reef,* it was, perhaps, at the expense of the ultimate significance of the novel, as in her failure to characterize fully Sophy Viner and Owen Leath. That *The Age of Innocence* is a shorter novel than either *The Custom of the Country* or *The House of Mirth* reveals the writer's discipline and her creation of a form absolutely suited to her subject. Seldom has this mastery of technique been equaled in a twentieth-century novel; and she reveals her abundant resources as a novelist most remarkably in marshaling the incidents of her plot, in writing dialogue with infinite nuances, in conceiving fully wrought characters, in controlling the point of view, and in maintaining a complex tone composed of irony and enthusiasm. She satirizes the rigidity and evasiveness of a society that she also respects, and she laughs ironically at human nature itself.

In writing *The Age of Innocence,* Wharton did not retreat from contemporary problems by celebrating a past culture and by focusing on technique, as some critics maintain. In a sense, she tried to escape the vexations of the postwar years by commemorating a culture that she had known as a child. She finally appreciated its stability, especially in view of the violence, flux, and dissolving standards that had marked the succeeding years. But the scope and complexity of the problems presented in the novel argue against those critics (including Stuart P. Sherman and Robert Morss Lovett on the committee that awarded it the Pulitzer Prize) who deplored its lack of contemporary relevance.[2] Granted that Wharton recreated a past culture with some reverence, she also saw that culture dispassionately; and she emphasized that its prejudices and problems still confronted America fifty years later, sometimes in more pressing guise. *The Age of Innocence* reveals a universal dimension as

Wharton comments upon the oppression of women by convention and their emancipation from it, the role of marriage and the family in determining the quality of a civilization, and, above all, the conflict between sexual passion and moral obligation.

Vernon Parrington was typical of the earlier critics who praised Wharton's artistry but criticized *The Age of Innocence* both for its lack of contemporary relevance and its failure to transcend the milieu that it mirrored[3] Such critics failed to see the connection between the New York of the 1870s and the America of the 1920s, but, as we must admit, Wharton herself did not explicitly stress this connection except in the epilogue. Later critics, including Blake Nevius, have discounted *The Age of Innocence* because it limits itself to an atypical segment of American society in the 1870s and does not reflect such current phenomena as the development of the labor movement, immigration from foreign lands, governmental corruption, the exploitation and waste of American resources, and the influence of the frontier.[4]

Surely any facet of society when recreated with verisimilitude and insight adds to an understanding of human nature; and such must have been Wharton's aim as a literary artist. In *The Age of Innocence* she developed the social, moral, and intellectual conflicts that had undermined the authority of the New York aristocracy in the 1870s, she mirrored their manners and conventions though she acknowledged their absurdity, she revealed a moral vision sensitive alike to the worth of tradition and the need for change, and she implied that the passing of a gracious order had its tragic as well as its inevitable aspects, much as Anton Chekhov had presented this theme in *The Cherry Orchard* and other plays. We can concede to her critics that Wharton in *The Age of Innocence* limited her subject, but we need not concede that it lacks significance as she developed it.

It is important to see that Archer's romantic idealizing of Paris is contrasted with the dark side of Ellen's experience there and her ambivalence about again leaving America. Wharton's fervently Francophile wartime writing here yields to a critical realism. Her linking of Newland Archer with Teddy Roosevelt argues against the assumption that his choice of New York over Paris was a destructive one or that Paris would necessarily have given him "the flower of life," which Wharton knows is seldom found and often unrecognized when found.

In discussing the structure of *The Age of Innocence,* Joseph Warren Beach observed that with few exceptions each chapter presents one scene, that each scene is pertinent to the central action, that nearly every scene has Archer as its focal presence, and that his mind interprets most of the action. Yet, for Beach, Archer himself never becomes the vital person that other characters in the novel do.[5] Actually, Archer could hardly have been presented as a strong and dominant character because Wharton conceived him as exemplifying a group of people who deliberately limited their experience and imagination because they were inhibited by tradition and by fear of criticism from their peers and also because they could place the needs of another above their own wishes. But if he is not a dominating presence, he is still a pervasive one in whom the conflicts presented in the novel center. Because Archer grows through his love for Ellen Olenska, Wharton emphasized the changes that occurred in him. The result is that the point-of-view character reveals an increasing complexity as the novel develops.

Wharton's maintenance of the single view, however, was not rigid; she frequently compared Archer's perspective with that of May Archer or Ellen Olenska, and more important, she supplemented his observations with authorial comment that was not limited by his unsuspected blindness to the world beyond his closed society. She also significantly utilized the viewpoints of secondary personages such as old Catherine Mingott, Sillerton Jackson, Larry Lefferts, and Monsieur Rivière. She stressed Archer's overt behavior and his interaction with the two women he loves as much as she did his deepening insight and the impact that his exclusive social group and his glimpses of a freer world outside have upon him. Certainly her concern with maintaining a single point of view in this novel was less absolute than James's, or her own in *The Reef*.

"Invincible innocence": The Social Panorama

New York society of the 1870s tended to confuse a cloistered virtue with respectability and even with morality, as we see in *The House of Mirth, The Reef,* and *Old New York*. As a constructive force, innocence, as Wharton regarded it, denoted the purity of those who followed a socially prescribed moral code that stressed fidelity and family loyalty in personal relationships within a restricted social class. For those who engaged in business, the code placed a commendable emphasis on probity rather than opportunism. Admirable as it was in many respects, this code, particularly in its personal aspects, had severe limitations. It was, at bottom, dishonest. Its adherents valued superficial pleasantness over a disturbing reality, they condemned those who did not conform to conventional patterns or who might threaten to change these patterns, and they cherished "respectability" and sound business practices more than the claims of individual liberty.

In the opening scene Newland Archer finds the "innocence" of May Welland, his betrothed, appealing. When he attends the opera with her, he assumes with approval that she cannot even recognize Faust's intent to seduce Margaret. But gradually he resents the probability that she will shut herself away from life, as her mother has, by refusing to become involved in the problems of others. Placid Mrs. Welland, in her "invincible innocence," excuses herself from listening to Ellen Olenska's troubles because she must keep her mind "bright and happy" for the sake of her slightly ailing husband. Even before Newland's marriage, he realizes with a shock that he does not want May to be like her mother. He wants more than Mrs. Welland's "innocence that seals the mind against imagination and the heart against experience"(*AI*, 45).

Although Archer is less naive than Mrs. Welland, he never fully recognizes his own conventionality. Considering himself capable of teaching May the value of music and books, he nevertheless has little interest in learning about the great world outside his own circle; and he finds comfort in the stability of New York society. Though he believes that cultural interests such as the opera have enlarged his mind, he is so limited by exclusive traditions that he expresses relief that the opera house is too small to accommodate the newly rich. He accepts the idea that all German texts of French operas sung by Swedish performers should be translated into Italian for American audiences—just as he accepts "all the other conventions on which his life was moulded." All aspects of Archer's life fall into settled patterns, and his indecisiveness prevents him from rebelling against those forces that constrict the spontaneous expression of the self and that encourage him to overlook evils demanding rectification. His conventionality is symbolized by the routine parting of his hair with two silver-backed brushes, the flower in his lapel, and his provincial pride in being a New Yorker, though he regards himself as cosmopolitan and fantasizes about the superiority of an intellectual and bohemian artistic life in Paris.

Wharton reveals Archer's limited views, subtly and ironically, at the very times that he is complacently evaluating, from the heights of his presumed sophistication, the limited views of others, particularly those of May. Charmed by Ellen Olenska's imagination and experience, he nevertheless reacts with hypocritical conservatism when he refuses to acknowledge her need to divorce a cruel and unfaithful husband. To openly recognize her bitter experience would be to acknowledge that a woman of his wife's family understands from wordly experience too much about sex. Archer's temptation to be unfaithful to May ultimately helps him achieve a greater honesty about himself; he is now able to recognize that passion and moral convention are sometimes strongly at odds. As a result of his admitting his own passions and his ultimate desire for an illicit affair with Ellen, he attains a degree of tolerance for those outside his own circle of complacent and morally "superior" aristocrats.

Regarding his relatives and friends as the whole world early in the book, he assumes that Ellen's naïveté prevents her from being impressed by the party that the Van der Luydens give for her. In Archer's circle, everyone recognizes that this party is the Van der Luydens' gesture of acceptance of Ellen—an acceptance reluctantly accorded by other aristocrats because she has returned to New York without her husband. As a matter of fact, Ellen's worldly knowledge makes her refuse to attach to the party the radical significance that Archer and his friends see in it. Ellen wants only to be accepted for what she is, not forgiven for something that is not her fault. Because Newland's friends still believe in the import of such social gestures, the farewell party that May gives for Ellen also assumes importance because for them it symbolizes the end of Newland's presumed affair with Ellen.

If he initially misjudges Ellen for her supposed inability to react according to his expectations at the time of the Van der Luydens' party, he also misjudges May by viewing her as more limited than she is. Before their marriage, he simply assumes that she will never be capable of surprising him with "a new idea, a weakness, a cruelty, or an emotion." Ironically, he is himself incapable at this time of recognizing her resentment of his affair with Mrs. Rushworth or her courage in suggesting that he marry his former mistress. He does not recognize the stratagems to which May resorts in order to keep him from leaving with Ellen, nor does he realize her lasting gratitude to him for giving up Ellen. His egocentric temperament, which limits his imagination, prevents him from seeing May as a woman instead of a stereotype. He fails to see that what he calls "her abysmal purity" is a myth largely of his own formulation—one that underestimates her intelligence, the extent of her worldly knowledge, her strength, and her capacity to fight for her interests.

Though May appears to Archer and her male contemporaries as an image of ethereal purity and as a helpless being, she is in Wharton's evaluation a woman of considerable strength. For one thing, May enjoys sports—at that time largely reserved for men. Twice Wharton refers to May's big, athletic hands—when May displays her ring and later when she tries dutifully to sit by her husband and do delicate needlework with hands meant for rowing and archery. May's interest in extending their honeymoon to Italy lies largely in the additional opportunities there to walk, ride, swim, and play tennis. Her skilled performance in "a feat of strength" at the Newport archery contest adds dimensions of competence and assurance to her character and aligns her, both in her apparently chaste temperament and in her prowess, with Diana. She also develops much resourcefulness when Ellen threatens to undermine her hold on Archer—a toughness and a tenacity of purpose that show she is more than the clinging, helpless woman so much cherished as the New York aristocrats' ideal.[6]

But the old ideals of these aristocrats are being threatened by a materialism represented in the novel by Julius Beaufort. As a new millionaire, he is tolerated because he has married an aristocratic old New York woman. Ineffectual and beautiful, his wife allows him to manage all details of their lavish ménage. When the public later condemns him for a speculation that causes financial loss to others, the aristocrats pity her but also censure her for looking to her family for help now that she has disastrously married outside her circle. The epilogue, however, reveals twenty-five years later that Beaufort has been able to "buy" a place in society and that his "bastard" is about to marry Archer's son without anyone's thinking twice about what would once have seemed presumptuous. If, in the victory of such parvenus, the naïveté, exclusiveness, and censoriousness of the aristocrats have weakened, the New York community is both better and worse for the change.

The matriarchal aristocrat Mrs. Manson Mingott links the stability of her class with the vigor and independence of the nouveau riche. Grotesque in her obesity, she manages, nevertheless, to be both regal and human, certainly more vigorous than her peers. She values highly the family ties and the concern for integrity that she sees in the aristocrats, but she also sees through their pretenses and their concern for propriety. No one dares gossip about her, even when she associates with Catholics, entertains opera singers, marries her daughters to foreigners, and has the first French windows in New York. In taking shortcuts around wearisome conventions early in the book, she aligns herself with Julius Beaufort; and she welcomes Mrs. Lemuel Struthers, "widow of Struthers' Shoe Polish," because new blood and new money are needed in New York society.

Symbolizing the most hypocritical aspects of the establishment, Sillerton Jackson and Lawrence Lefferts become censorious, unsympathetic observers of the scene around them. Old Jackson damns with innuendo; for when he says, "Anyhow, he—eventually—married her," the pause surrounding "eventually" speaks volumes. He is uncharitable about Ellen because her mother years before had broken with custom by allowing Ellen to wear black satin at her debut. Even more offensive is young Lefferts, who is perpetually in Sillerton's company and is, if anything, still more cynical. The tight society, for which they are spokesmen, encourages slanderous gossip precisely because it embalms so perfectly its own traditions and the life histories of its members. At the same time, these two men are insensitive to the generous aspects of these same traditions.

"A hieroglyphic world": Irony, Symbol, and Image

Wharton's imagery, symbolism, ironic intonations, and stylistic assurance in *The Age of Innocence* resulted in a more perfectly wrought and modulated work than *The Custom of the Country*. Viola Hopkins Winner notes that Wharton used an ordered style in the novel to satirize the somewhat artificial order of a conventionalized society.[7] She expressed her ironic vision in a supple prose capable of a spectrum of effects that range from derision to dry but amiable comedy. She frequently employed parallel construction and the artfully balanced sentence that ends with a satirical twist: "But the Beauforts were not exactly common; some people said they were even worse" (*AI*, 16); "People had always been told that the house at Skuytercliff was an Italian villa. Those who had never been to Italy believed it; so did some who had" (*AI*, 128). Often the irony inheres in one word that is more serious—or less so—than its context, as the "mildly" in the statement describing Archer's affair with Mrs. Rushworth—her charms "had held his fancy through two mildly agitated years" (*AI*, 5).

Wharton's ironic vision throughout the novel keeps the affair between Archer and Ellen from attaining proportions of high tragedy, except briefly in Archer's own mind. Frustration as much as heartbreak marks their final separation. Consequently, Wharton envisioned most of the love scenes with a measured objectivity, aware at once of an intense seriousness in Archer's passion as well as of the difficulties in the way of its consummation. An embarrassing interruption or an unconsciously comic remark or gesture characteristically deflates the romantic and glamorous aspects of this relationship; for, as Blake Nevius notes, the lovers are almost never afforded privacy in their meetings. When Archer anticipates a secret tryst in Ellen's apartment, he arrives to find the coats of several other invited guests in the hallway. At one point, on sudden impulse, he kisses her satin-slippered foot with a degree of romantic extravagance uncharacteristic of him. Later, he kisses a pink umbrella, mistakenly assuming it to be hers. On an impulse, he goes to Boston for a furtive talk with her and finds a secluded dining room, only to be joined by an entourage of schoolteachers. When he makes elaborate excuses to May to prepare for a business trip to Washington, where he will be able to see Ellen alone, Ellen's grandmother has a stroke, she is called home, and he can only expect to pass her train going in the other direction. Even when Archer finds himself alone with Ellen in a carriage after May delegates him to drive her to her stricken grandmother, he is distracted because he is making love to Ellen in a carriage that belongs to his wife.

Early in the novel the narrator comments that the aristocrats "lived in a kind of hieroglyphic world, where the real thing was never said or done or even thought, but only represented by a set of arbitrary signs" (*AI, 42*). Wharton attaches many such signs to single objects that thereby acquire a ritualistic or arcane meaning. They include the restoration of position to the Beauforts that is implied by Mrs. Mingott's carriage parked outside their door; the social acceptance of Ellen implied by the white envelope handed through the door by someone who had arrived in the Van der Luydens' carriage; and the bride's collection of three dozen of everything, monogrammed, to imply that traditional expectations are being met. A ballroom in one's house is an incontrovertible symbol of status that serves to elevate one parvenu family over another.

Objects also serve in the novel as a symbolic means of characterizing individuals. May's satin and lace wedding dress suggests both her love of the traditional and her practicality, because she plans to have a gown that she can wear two years. Mrs. Mingott's cream-colored house in a period of brownstones connotes her mild rebelliousness, and Ellen's peeling stucco house suggests her poverty. Ellen's black dress of fluid cut and low neckline, May's white dress undergirded by whalebone, Ellen's red roses, and May's lilies of the valley symbolize Archer's views of these women. Ellen is for him a woman of lush sexuality; May, a woman of virginal purity.

Wharton not only employs objects as symbols to communicate with the reader but also presents them as forces that control individuals. For example, the Welland house with its heavy carpets, watchful servants, and stacks of invitations and cards on a hall table exerts a tyrannizing effect upon Archer's spirit and suggests the restrictive aspects of his culture. The Welland way of life, like a debilitating drug, makes any existence that is less affluent and conventional seem "unreal and precarious." Objects in his mother's home produce a similar comforting, but anesthetizing, effect on Archer. In her dining room the candlelit portraits in dark frames on dark walls suggest to him a reverence for ancestors and a willingness only to half-see reality.

Wharton uses entire scenes, as well as objects, with symbolic intent. For example, the Van der Luydens' party and May's farewell dinner both signify, as we have noted, society's pronouncements on Ellen's fate. Another important scene, rich in implication, occurs when Ellen endeavors to establish for Archer a philosophical perspective on the end of their love affair. They meet for the last time in the antiquities room of the Metropolitan Museum of Art. The intensity of their present conflict contrasts with the passivity of the artifacts in this room—mummies, statuary, and other objects of art and daily use—though these artifacts are also the material evidence of human struggles that have long since transpired. Ellen, standing before a case of such objects labeled "Use Unknown," reflects upon the "cruel" truth that eventually nothing matters—nothing does, in fact, matter after a few years to any human being. A museum guard, "like a ghost stalking through a necropolis," walks down the vista of mummies and sarcophagi and interrupts Archer when he suggests to Ellen that they elope. Throughout this scene references to the "Gorgon" as a reality symbol are abundant, an image discussed below.

Another scene early in the novel achieves notable symbolic intonations—the scene in which the Archers call on the Van der Luydens in a kind of pilgrimage to gain help from them as the arbiters of their social class. The elderly Van der Luydens and their compatriots have little vitality; for them the ceremonious is everything. They symbolize, in fact, the deadness of the conventions that attempt to preserve intact the values whose efficacy has long ago disappeared. A servant appears to answer the door as if awakened from the dead, the drawing room is "enshrouded," and the Van der Luyden banquets all loom as funereal in Archer's memory. To him, Mrs. Van der Luyden's rosy cheeks suggest a corpse caught in a glacier and preserved for ages. The scene also conveys the exaggerated importance accorded these social leaders and the real, though irrelevant, power they exercise. Images related to the regal dominate when Mrs. Van der Luyden smilingly approaches her husband, like Esther seeking out King Ahasuerus, to persuade him to stage a party for Ellen.

Wharton also makes abundant use of stylistic images to intensify the effects at which she aims. She satirizes inflated social conventions largely by means of images associated with the tribal or the anthropological. Ellen's farewell dinner is a "tribal rally around a kinswoman about to be eliminated from the tribe" (*AI*, 337), the Grace Church wedding is a ritual seemingly of ancient vintage dating "from the dawn of history," and the secrecy surrounding the wedding journey is a "sacred taboo of the prehistoric ritual" (*AI*, 179–80).

To convey her sympathy for Archer, she resorts to nightmare images that threaten physical danger and emphasize his torturous uncertainties whenever he thinks of leaving May for Ellen. He sees himself, as Viola Hopkins Winner indicates, "on the edge of a steep precipice about to pitch headlong into darkness" (*AI*, 174), as "adrift far off in the unknown" (*AI*, 186), as in a "black abyss . . . sinking deeper and deeper" (*AI*, 187), as "clinging to the edge of a sliding precipice" (*AI*, 254), as "having slipped through the meshes of time and space" (*AI*, 231), and as existing on "the edge of a vortex"(*AI*, 245).

Wharton makes striking use of the Gorgon image to intimate the uncertainties facing the lovers, their inability to confront certain kinds of reality, and their impatience to break through conventions to attain another kind of reality. In the museum sequence, Ellen asserts that she has found a kind of salvation by submitting to the Gorgon, a mythical figure who fastens the eyelids open so that one can never again rest in "blessed darkness." As a reward for facing the truth, the Gorgon dries one's tears. Ellen accordingly prevails upon Archer to return home to May and to face reality; but, until after the farewell dinner and May's announcement of her pregnancy, he cannot quite face the full implications of his situation.

If the scope of *The Age of Innocence* is narrower than that customarily expected in the works of realists of the 1920s, it would be hard to find a book in which the problems of a group of people at a certain time are more carefully perceived, their manners and conventions more meticulously documented and criticized, the tenuous balance between the values of innocence and of experience more tolerantly analyzed, and the conflicts between tradition and change more memorably dramatized.

Chapter Six
Novellas and Short Stories

The Novella: The "third, and intermediate, form of tale—the long short story"

Wharton's published works include eighty-six short stories, thirteen novellas, and fourteen novels. Beginning in 1900, she published regularly in all three genres until the last years of her life almost forty years later. Even earlier than this, she had produced two novellas not published until many years after their completion: the novella written before her fifteenth birthday, *Fast and Loose* (published in 1977), a remarkably enjoyable and satiric work; and *Bunner Sisters*, written in the early 1890s and published in 1916.

In *The Writing of Fiction,* Wharton discusses at length the differences between the novel and the short story. The story emphasizes situation; the novel emphasizes characterization. The story must have a strong beginning and ending and stress compactness and immediacy, whereas the novel can develop more characters and in greater complexity. More generally, she argues for the basic Jamesian principles of unity of point of view and clear continuity in the passage of time, and she acknowledges her debt to French and Russian writers of fiction. In spite of the frequency with which she turned to the novella form, she seems not to have considered it critically as a genre separate in characteristics (other than obvious length) from either the short story or the novel. In *The Writing of Fiction* she devotes only one parenthetical sentence to this genre: "Meanwhile, it may be pointed out that a third, and intermediate, form of tale—the *long* short story—is available for any subject too spreading for conciseness yet too slight in texture to be stretched into a novel" (*WF,* 44). It seems not inconceivable that Wharton produced her large number of novellas, in part, by accident when a story grew too long or when a novel needed a sharper focus and more attention to action, although she maintained that authors should choose between story and novel form as soon as they begin a work of fiction.

Wharton's novellas differ widely in subject and treatment, although several of them deal with problems relating to sex and marriage, the breaking of conventions, and the ramifications of such actions. The principal figure in *The Touchstone* (1900), Glennard, obtains money for his marriage to Alexa by selling letters written to him by Margaret Aubyn, an established novelist who has died several years after leaving New England to live in Europe. Although she knew that Glennard would remain only a friend, the novelist writes passionate letters to him, as if driven to expose her shame—pursuing a man who did not want her. Before she left, he himself had experienced a kind of shame or embarrassment in her presence because he felt inferior to a woman of talent and also because he was not aroused sexually by her appearance—her long, pale face and her nearsighted eyes. Although he never reveals publicly that he was the recipient of the letters or that he was the dealer who profited from their sale to a press, he suffers guilt after the volume becomes a best-seller and when he hears readers condemn the unworthy man Aubyn faithfully loved or the man who exposed her pitiful letters to thousands of readers.

Although the guilt of Glennard is central to the narrative, unexpected interest arises from other aspects of the novella. Glennard confesses his guilt to Alexa, who in turn feels guilty because her marriage and their financial status have come at the expense of Margaret's memory. Glennard, now reading Margaret's letters, finds himself no longer feeling inferior to her but drawn to the woman he rejected. He now finds "all that was feminine in her, the quality he had always missed."[1] His belated guilt and sexual arousal anticipate Wharton's frequent use, in later novellas, stories, and novels, of the theme of the woman returning from the dead to claim her lover who has married, to arouse debilitating guilt in him, and to haunt him—either out of continuing love or a desire for vengeance. Glennard's belated love for his dead first wife also suggests the dilemma later dramatized in *The Fruit of the Tree*.

Sanctuary (1903) has been viewed negatively by critics because of its implausible central situation. Kate Orme, shocked by the moral failure of her fiancé, Denis Peyton, marries him, forces him to confess his shortcomings publicly, and then dedicates her life to counteracting his evil influence over their offspring. Kate is shamed by his public confession that he defrauded a relative, who then drowned herself and her child. She is further shamed upon learning that her father had successfully covered up a crime and felt no misgivings about doing so. Though she herself is not guilty, she feels ashamed of her association with both men and responds penitently in positive acts of contrition. She is not masochistic and is never quite overwhelmed by her situation. Her reward comes when her son as a young adult withstands severe temptation, having avoided the taint of his father and grandfather and become a sensitive and morally responsible young man. Despite the implausibility of her being able to implement her goal, Kate convinces the reader of her strength and of her willingness to face embarrassment candidly and to shoulder responsibility for salvaging some good from a morally dubious situation after the discovery of the perfidy of both her fiancé and her father.

Madame de Treymes, an attempt by Wharton to produce a Jamesian novella, is one of her most carefully polished works. In it, a young American living in France, Fanny Malrive, relinquishes her freedom to marry her American lover rather than risk losing custody of her son to her divorced husband's relatives. The unscrupulous Madame de Treymes has sought to negotiate the situation for her own financial benefit and that of her lover. *The Marne,* though sentimental, holds interest because of its surprising use of the ghost figure at the close of a story about a young soldier and because of its satire of civilians who enjoy the flamboyant drama of patriotic fund raising and rallies. Like the later novel *A Son at the Front,* this novella is dedicated to Ronald Simmons, an American soldier who was Wharton's friend and had been killed shortly before she wrote *The Marne.*

Old New York (1924) is more than a collection of four separate novellas (*False Dawn, The Old Maid, New Year's Day,* and *The Spark*). Wharton sought to connect the four as a series of illuminations of scenes and attitudes in old New York over four decades of the nineteenth century. Giving a degree of unity to the volume, three of the novellas employ the same educated Harvard man as narrator; names and places are repeated from one narrative to the next; and an ironic tone remains fairly constant throughout the four novellas. *The Old Maid* sold more separate copies than did the other three, and became a successful stage play and motion picture. Wharton initially had difficulty in securing its magazine publication, however, because of its sympathetic treatment of an unmarried mother, her failure to reveal her previous pregnancy to her fiancé, and the successful concealing of the daughter's illegitimacy for two decades. It contains Wharton's best portrayal of an intense and prolonged struggle for dominance between two women, Charlotte Lovell and her cousin Delia Ralston.

In *Her Son* (1933) a widow searches across Europe for the illegitimate son she and her lover had given away secretly before they married and had another son. After her husband's death, the second son dies at the age of twenty-two, and she begins the exhausting search for her firstborn. She has no means of positively identifying the man she has not seen since infancy, and she is thus fair game for anyone who wishes to exploit her efforts. The novella, written when Wharton was over seventy, shows Wharton's ability to sustain a believable character in an unbelievable quest.

Three of Wharton's novellas demand special attention because they reveal her insight into the problems of the poor in rural, small-town, and urban environments and because they were written by Wharton at different times in her career and in widely varying circumstances.

Novellas about the Poor: "Without an Added Ornament"

Bunner Sisters (written 1891; published 1916), *Ethan Frome* (1911), and *Summer* (1917) provide instances of Wharton's experimentation with widely differing characters, settings, and structural patterns. In them, she focuses upon the lives of the poor; and she poignantly demonstrates how they must settle for frustration and survival. All three works are haunted by death. In each an isolated individual experiences brief ecstasy in love and then suffers severe loss.

A character in each novella takes responsibility for someone else, even at the expense of his or her own well-being and regardless of whether or not the person helped is deserving or lovable. The central figures in these books do not achieve mastery; they merely learn to endure. The fact that people in constricted situations may prove themselves selfless is the only solace that Wharton offers, but some people, such as Charity Royall in *Summer,* do not progress even that far. If anything, characters motivated by unselfishness and a sense of responsibility suffer more than the selfish and irresponsible. In these books life begins unhappily for the deprived, they move through "crucial moments" of intense suffering, and they simply continue to live after the single drama of life for them has dissipated. Neither villains nor heroes emerge in these novellas. Although comic touches abound, they are sardonic and deepen the mood.

Bunner Sisters takes place in New York City, whereas the setting for *Ethan Frome* and *Summer* is rural Massachusetts near Wharton's home, The Mount. In these two narratives Wharton sought, as she declared in *A Backward Glance,* "to draw life as it really was" and to correct the romantic impressions left by the "rose-and-lavender" pages of Mary E. Wilkins Freeman and Sarah Orne Jewett (*BG,* 293–94). In 1922, Wharton explained that such New England writers had used the colorful flora and the homespun dialect of their region but had ignored the granite protruding through the grass. Accordingly, she emphasized in *Ethan Frome* the rigors of life in a harsh land, with its rocky soil, its cold winters, and its bleak, desolate beauty.[2] In *Summer* she analyzed the stifling effects of New England even upon Charity Royall, who loves its landscape.

Because Wharton painstakingly strove for truth of impression in these New England tales, she took issue with critics who assumed that she could write authentically only about aristocratic New York. In *A Backward Glance* she recalls that in 1911 she read *Ethan Frome* to Walter Berry as she wrote it and that together they scrutinized the milieu of the tale for accuracy (*BG,* 296). She established her authority to write about the rural scene on the basis of her ten-year residence in Lenox, her daily excursions into the countryside, and her conversations with a clergyman who ministered to the Bear Mountain community a few miles from her home (this settlement served as the prototype for Charity Royall's birthplace).

More to the point is her consistently demonstrated ability to depict people whose daily routines and circumstances are different from her own and to recreate the life of earlier generations, whether in Italy, New York, or western Massachusetts. Whether she accurately judged how much Ethan would have charged to drive the narrator, how much he would have known about alimony and bank loans, and how the community dances in the village were staged all matter less than her insight into the psychological effects of rural isolation, her knowledge, as an avid gardener, of the patience demanded of those who work with unproductive soil, and her empathy, as one at that moment preparing for divorce, with Ethan's compulsion to escape a deadening marriage. She knew from living with a sick and difficult spouse that pettiness and anger, more often than nobility, are the results of suffering. The contrast between the beauty of the landscape around Lenox and the "mental starvation" of the people who inhabited it disturbed her.[3]

Observing carefully the people living near her and their surroundings, Wharton recognized that the telephone and automobile had made their lives fuller than those of their parents. Thus both *Ethan Frome* and *Summer,* by design, reflect the deprivations of the preceding generation.

The Harsh Artistry of *Ethan Frome*

In *Ethan Frome* Wharton emphasizes the differences between the present and the recent past by using a young narrator, who must look back twenty-five years. Distressed by the duration into late spring of snow drifts and intense cold, he imagines himself in the place of these people in the recent past when hardship was even more acute and isolation more complete. Twenty-eight during the main part of the story, in the engineer's retrospective narrative Ethan is already fifty-two and prematurely aged by toil and by the bitter climate when the narrator first sees him.

Isolated from the world, Ethan Frome's wife, Zeena, naturally chooses to be sick because sickness promises adventure in its possible complications, sudden cures, and relapses. The patent medicines she receives in the mail provide her only excitement and her only relief from a paralyzing spiritual monotony. She resents Mattie Silver's vitality and her tendency to daydream more than she fears Ethan's interest in her. Zeena is tired and "needs" household help, but Mattie, the hired girl, lacks efficiency. Zeena is not simply ? part of Ethan's curse, as some critics have implied, but a deprived woman who grieves over lost beauty when the cherished red pickle dish she has saved since her wedding is used by Mattie and broken.

The book is fraught with such ironies: the dish that is treasured is the one that is broken; the pleasure of the one solitary meal that Ethan and Mattie share ends in distress; the ecstasy of the coasting ends in suffering; the moment of dramatic renunciation when Ethan and Mattie choose suicide rather than elopement ends not in glorious death but in years of pain. The lovely Mattie Silver becomes an ugly, querulous woman cared for by Zeena, who, again ironically, finds strength and companionship by caring for her former rival.

Wharton's strenuous attempt to counteract the "rose-and-lavender" impression of New England that she found in works by Mary E. Wilkins Freeman and Sarah Orne Jewett, and her refusal to present her people triumphant over their incessant struggles alienated critics including John Crowe Ransom, Bernard DeVoto, and Lionel Trilling, who recoiled in particular from *Ethan Frome* and who contended that Wharton excited a reader's sadistic sensibilities.[4] They are so uncomfortable with her objectivity that they gain little esthetic and spiritual satisfaction from the book. Instead, they imply that *Ethan Frome* is distinctive for the technical skill that Wharton displayed in it rather than for its vision of human experience. But, if critics are to value these novellas as literature, they cannot admire their technical dexterity to the exclusion of their truth to the human experience Wharton dramatized in them.

During her lifetime, the popularity of *Ethan Frome*, perhaps the best-known of her books, caused Wharton some dissatisfaction. She opposed those who insisted that it was her best work. Nevertheless, she regarded the book as the fruition of her long search for technical mastery and artistic maturity and contended that she had carefully modulated her structure to the requirements of her materials. The characterization is subtle, strong, and masterful. Her three chief figures achieve a mythic dimension and seem to be extensions of the grim landscape itself. The ardent lover turned cynic, the beautiful woman turned soured cripple, and the protective mother figure emerging as a sinister dictatorial presence are all illuminating and arresting conceptions. The very texture of the prose elicits admiration, particularly the accomplished use of imagery to sustain a moral judgment or to comment implicitly on a character or situation. The blighted apple trees, the rocks protruding from the soil, the neglected cemetery, the broken cut-glass pickle dish that was a wedding present too good to use, the false teeth that Ethan hates to see beside Zeena's bed, the misshapen remodeled farmhouse that reminds the narrator of Ethan's crippled back—all are vivid and compelling metaphors in this tale of spiritual deprivation. Yet these deprivations, endured stoically, form the vision of life that the story creates. We cannot, then, separate the technical felicities of the novel—its compelling characterization and its vital imagery—from the experience that Wharton sought to enlarge in the work.

Because life was stark rather than rich for her characters, Wharton felt that she must avoid the leisurely elaboration inherent in the novel form and utilize instead the bluntness possible in short fiction. Writing an introduction to a new edition of *Ethan Frome* in 1922, she realized that this conviction conflicted with her usual view that the novel provided the most appropriate genre for any narrative spreading over two generations. In the case of this narrative, she had instinctively realized that the shorter form could alone express the unadorned strength of Ethan Frome and that exhaustive analysis would tend to nullify the stark effect for which she was striving. To encompass Ethan's situation persuasively, she saw that she must present it "without an added ornament, or a trick of drapery or lighting" (*EF*, vi–vii).

In the earliest version of *Ethan Frome,* written in French, she used no character as narrator. In the final version, the narrator provides a frame for the story and a complicated time scheme through which the author could dramatically contrast the bleak existence of her characters in the present with their youthful expectations in the past. More sophisticated than the people he observes, he learns gradually about the tragedy from several simple, relatively inarticulate persons; each of the villagers tells him as much about the situation as he can understand. His more sophisticated intelligence, then, synthesizes these complicated and mysterious fragments into a single *vision*—an imaginative story—that gives order to the myriad facts and impressions that others have provided. Possessing "scope enough to see it all," he is, in effect, a kind of artist in his own right. His own character is important in helping him to fulfill his task. He is never the factual reporter; he is the curious, meditative, expansive sensibility who feels ready sympathy for the wasted Ethan Frome when he first observes him and who associates the bleakness in Ethan's face with his own reaction to the harsh winter. In his endeavors to withstand the benumbing influence of coldness and isolation upon his own spirit, he finds strength in actively sympathizing with Ethan, Zeena, and Mattie. His human warmth, perhaps, prevents his own spiritual relapse.

As an engineer who constantly daydreams, he can identify with Ethan, who had attended a technical school and who had found the beginnings of a sustaining illusion in his work in the laboratories. But, as an outsider and a member of another generation, he is remote enough from Ethan's tragedy to see it in perspective, much as it appalls him. His seeing Ethan's youthful promise at a distance deepens the implications of his tragedy because time only dulls Ethan's wounds but does not cure them. He has had to learn to endure, and time has only accentuated his suffering instead of alleviating it. Because the tragedy continues to ramify from the past into the present through the sensibilities of an imaginative narrator, mundane survival for Ethan and Mattie becomes more horrible in its impact than their sudden death would have been. As a result of their accident, following their suicide pact, Mattie and Ethan exchange a hoped for life-in-death for a demeaning death-in-life when their attempt fails. How overwhelming their defeat has been Wharton fully actualizes by presenting it obliquely through the eyes of a young stranger.[5]

Summer: "Confusedly . . . what might be the sweetness of dependence"

In *Summer,* as in *Ethan Frome,* the principal character, Charity Royall, aspires to escape from a stultifying community. She has a brief love affair, faces pregnancy alone, and eventually resigns herself, at least temporarily, to a life of emotional barrenness as the bride of her elderly guardian. Unlike Ethan, Charity lacks any sense of responsibility or affection for those with whom she lives, and she remains in North Dormer because she cannot otherwise survive. She never contends against nature as a hostile force, as Ethan does, but identifies with it as a source of moral and spiritual strength, rather than with people. Nature reinforces her assurance early in the book and sustains her in her later desperation. She responds to it with ecstasy, savoring the roughness of the dry mountain grass on her skin, the smell of thyme crushed against her face, and the songs of birds. She lies in the grass "immersed in an inarticulate well-being," reaches out to the light of the morning sun when she wakes, and feels her turbulent spirit at one with the storms. Within herself, she knows that she is part of a larger universe through this affinity with the physical world surrounding her.

Others in North Dormer, a village two blocks long, do not share this mystical exaltation. Not only are the land and climate characterized by rigor; so also are the standards that regulate the social existence of its people. Class lines are even more inhibiting for them when they wish to marry than such barriers would be in high urban society. The double standard for sexual behavior is sometimes devastating in this claustrophobic village. There, people cannot escape the circumstances of their birth and heredity or the traditions that enclose them. The mountain that looms threateningly over those who, like Charity, leave its alienated group of outcasts to live in North Dormer is symbolic of the inhibiting forces of rural tradition and inflexible ancestral ways. Those who suffer most from alienation often intensify their own isolation; such is the paradox informing the lives of the mountain people who refuse to admit strangers from the village below to their homes and who inspire distrust in all who approach.

Lawyer Royall, Charity's guardian, has intellectual curiosity and a thirst for knowledge—attributes that she does not share and tends to scorn. Royall's past emerges through the villagers' shadowy allusions to his drinking, his interest in women, and his premature retirement from a city practice. An intelligent but lonely widower whose wistful interest in a young woman somewhat resembles Ethan's in Mattie, Royall is nevertheless distinguished by his jealousy, his drunken temper, and his associating with disreputable women in the city. He arouses Charity's hostility as she grows up. Not an intellectual, she identifies books only by their covers, considers the public library where she works a prison, and finds bewildering the historical interests of her lover, Harney, an architect who spends a summer in the village. Royall is the most powerful man in town, but he is powerless whenever he faces Charity's rebellion or determination. She feels hatred and sexual revulsion for him, and she enjoys dominating him. She asserts her cool authority in other ways; for example, when she enters the public library to begin her work, she insolently plants her hat on the bust of Minerva.

But Charity is vulnerable to sexual passion, and her assurance diminishes the first afternoon she meets Harney: "Confusedly, the young man . . . had made her feel for the first time what might be the sweetness of dependence." She allows herself to drift with the force of passion, and eventually she must endure the humiliation of Harney's deserting her and of learning that he is to marry a woman of his own class. Pregnant, Charity seeks help wherever she can hope to find it, first from an abortionist, whose assistant confiscates her money and only piece of jewelry, and then from the inhabitants of the mountain village where she hopes to find her mother, a prostitute whose face she cannot recall. Symbolically, her mother deserts her instead of helping her; she dies in the most sordid surroundings just before Charity arrives. The body lies discolored and bloated on an unmade cot while boisterous drunks blaspheme nearby. Charity meets Royall on her long walk back to town; and, now that she feels cornered by fate, she agrees to marry him. She faintly acknowledges that he is being kind.

The surface plot follows that of popular sentimental fiction, but its significance strikes deeper. Wharton presents the cliché situation of an independent adolescent brought to maturity by a tempestuous love affair, humbled by her lover's desertion, and saved from an abortion and social ostracism by a stable citizen whom she has previously scorned. But Charity's development represents no moral improvement, for she gains nothing in human sensitivity and continues to prefer nature to humanity. Her confidence and freedom from inhibition in the past arose from the detachment with which she viewed others. When she loses this objectivity, she only becomes confused about their human attributes and her own. Even her decision against an abortion is a last-moment reassertion of her independence: she rebels against the pressures of a judgmental society. She insists upon keeping what is hers, just as the bird's nest and the warm grass have been hers. She is motivated by an animistic sense that the fetus growing within her links her with the forces of nature—a universe bigger than North Dormer; and, at the very least, the developing life gives her importance in her own eyes. She is in reality a child of nature, and she regards her unborn child with the protectiveness of a wild animal. But her decision to keep the baby forces her into marriage with a man she has despised, though he is her moral superior in compassion. The age of her guardian, his drinking, and the overtones of incest ominously darken the ending of the story.

Charity's love affair in effect costs her her independence as a human being. She has, so to speak, spent her life in one summer. Her passion—beautiful, wild, and brief—exists in memory only as the Fourth of July celebration to which Harney took her. That celebration of independence ended in her driving back with Harney to an unchanged village where the independence she sought was impossible. Similarly, after their marriage, Charity and Royall drive back in cold autumn moonlight. Her summer experience made her aware of the potential that emotion holds for a mature woman. In exchange, she lost an inner self-reliance that would have ensured her human survival and possibly her escape from both North Dormer and the implacable cosmic forces symbolized by the mountain—forces with which she is in large measure attuned but which also represent a fatality far stronger than she as a limited individual can cope with.[6]

Bunner Sisters: "the inutility of sacrifice"

Underlying the *Bunner Sisters* are two themes: the sinister nature of poverty, and the ironically tragic consequences of unselfish behavior. In illustration of these themes, Ann Eliza Bunner gives up her own suitor and her small savings to her sister, Evelina. Because no act of love is totally selfless, Ann Eliza assumes that, as her reward, she will share vicariously in her sister's happiness. Instead, Evelina becomes more remote in her new, presumed affluence; she moves away, and she is condescending and impersonal in her occasional letters.

Wharton's sense of the unusual implications of her materials intensifies continually as the tale moves to its tragic denouement. Instead of happiness, Evelina experiences misery in her marriage, and her health fails under the strain. After the broken Evelina returns home, the thought crosses Ann Eliza's mind that she may now completely possess her sister's affection and companionship. But even this modicum of happiness is denied her when she learns that Evelina is a convert to Roman Catholicism and will, Ann Eliza assumes, now be separated from her for eternity.

More isolated than ever before, Ann Eliza feels herself a victim of the irrational forces that control the universe and of the unpredictable aspects of human life and human emotions. She had previously thought the universe was controlled by predictable moral principles, one of which was the value of self-sacrifice. The identification of herself as the cause of the tragedy and of the ever-widening gulf between herself and Evelina deepens her sense of alienation and desolation. Ann Eliza's final realization that all her previous beliefs had been mistaken is convincing aesthetically because Wharton meticulously emphasizes Ann Eliza's naïveté in her every word, act, and thought; and her naïveté is intensified by a certain recklessness and lack of critical sense.[7]

This novella is only a partial success, its stilted dialogue and the obtrusive presence of the author marking it as an early work. But Wharton's growing artistry is manifest in the exactitude of the details she uses to depict the uneventful lives of women who barely survive as shopkeepers, dressmakers, or milliners. She does achieve notable effects—a consistency of tone, for example, reinforcing her conviction that, for the deprived of this world, the ramifications of one unintended or unwise conversation can lead ultimately to a catastrophe out of all proportion to its inciting cause. For the poor, there exists no margin for error.

The Short Story: "A shaft driven straight into the heart of experience"

Edith Wharton's artistry in the short story is subtler and her imaginative reach greater than her own somewhat prescriptive literary theory might lead us to expect. In *The Writing of Fiction* she sets forth her views on the form of a good short story by emphasizing its directness: it must not be a web loosely drawn over many aspects of life but "a shaft driven straight into the heart of experience." In her view, all fiction develops through the separating of "crucial instances" from the general run of experience, but the short story exacts from its author even more skill in recognizing and interpreting such moments of significance. The author must introduce no irrelevant detail to distract the reader's attention for a moment. The effect of compactness and instantaneousness, she thought, would result from the strict observation of the unity of time and from the use of a single pair of eyes to focus upon the rapidly enacted episodes. The establishing of a vital, vivid impression, she asserted, is imperative to ensure the reader's vicarious presence in the milieu or his identification with the conflict presented. The beginning of a short story, therefore, stretches a writer's resources more than the conclusion.

For the story, even more than for the novel, the artist's selection from human experience and the reduction of its chaotic aspects to some sort of order are indispensable. Throughout her career, Wharton reiterated these two principles; and she increased her emphasis upon them as experimental writers became fascinated with the "stream of consciousness" and as naturalist writers concentrated on revealing a "slice of life." Her own stories manifest her conviction that art cannot simply reflect life; artists must refine upon their own experience by turning their materials about and by focusing them until exactly the right light refracts through them. Effective economy arises naturally when authors are so imbued with their subject that they feel no temptation to decorate its surface with adventitious elements that might be interesting in themselves but not crucial.

Her careful ordering of detail enabled Wharton to attain in many of her shorter works a psychological complexity in characterization that is ordinarily to be found only in the novel. In her short stories she usually illuminates, rather than resolves, the refractory situations that she subjects to her scrutiny. The significance of her characters and events often ranges beyond the literal into the realm of the universal. Wharton's endeavor to develop exhaustively certain important aspects of experience often led her beyond the short story to the novella, a form that while offering greater opportunities for revealing character still imposed some limitation on the number of persons and episodes involved.

Characteristically, her best tales reveal extraordinary psychological and moral insight; and they achieve distinction through her exploration of human situations of considerable complexity. Most of the stories, first published in magazines, were reprinted in the eleven collections that Wharton compiled between 1899 and 1937; but the stories appeared constantly throughout her career, beginning in 1891. One third of them appeared before her first great novel, *The House of Mirth,* and were mostly reprinted in three collections: *The Greater Inclination* (1899), *Crucial Instances* (1901), and *The Descent of Man* (1904).

These early works include efforts as distinguished and as varied in theme and tone as "A Journey," "Souls Belated," "The Mission of Jane," "The Other Two," "The Quicksand," and "The Lady's Maid's Bell." The chief characteristic marking them as early work—a tendency toward the epigrammatic—slows the pace. Dialogue is marked by virtuosity, and authorial comment diverts attention from the dramatic intensity of the "crucial instances." The early stories for the most part do not fully attain the depth and complexity of her later work. Yet the themes she most often explores in them are those that dominate her subsequent fiction: the mystery of the supernatural, the development of the artist, and the nature and role of women in society.

She finished the second third of her brief fiction by 1916 and collected it in *The Hermit and the Wild Woman* (1908), *Tales of Men and Ghosts* (1910), and *Xingu* (1916). "The Eyes," a chilling indictment of a man's sinister nature, and "Xingu," a delightfully amusing satire on intellectual pretension, represent only two of her outstanding contributions to this genre from her middle period.

The final third of her stories appeared after World War I and include many of her finest: "Miss Mary Pask," "Bewitched," "Atrophy," "A Bottle of Perrier," "After Holbein," "The Day of the Funeral," "Joy in the House," "Pomegranate Seed," and "Roman Fever." These she published in *Here and Beyond* (1926), *Certain People* (1930), *Human Nature* (1933), and *The World Over* (1936). Her last volume, *Ghosts* (1937), contained only one previously uncollected tale (the excellent "All Souls"), and it is the only collection limited to stories of one type and containing a preface by the author. Though masterful short fiction appeared in every period of Wharton's long career she may have reached the peak of her skill in this genre in the 1920s and 1930s.

Finding Women's Place

In roughly thirty of her stories, as well as in several of her novels and novellas, Wharton examined the role and status of women, the implications of marriage as seen through the eyes of a woman, the relationship between mother and child, and the rapidly changing views about divorce and about liaisons outside of marriage. Though she explored these subjects insistently, she approached the issues from varying angles and arrived at contradictory conclusions. If any consistent pattern of conviction emerges from the stories, which cover almost fifty years, it is that each woman must decide for herself what is best in her own situation. When Wharton began writing, divorce in many parts of America spelled disgrace not only to the divorcée but to her relatives; yet divorce was commonplace only a few years later. Views on love affairs outside marriage changed much more slowly. In any event, it is remarkable that in the 1890s and even at the turn of the century a woman from Wharton's conservative milieu could examine so vigorously and so searchingly issues related to divorce and to love, legal or illicit. Certainly no American author before 1930 produced such penetrating studies of women who, instead of marrying, decide to risk social ostracism by contracting temporary alliances based on mutual trust and sexual desire.

In other stories from this early period, Wharton deplores the fact that women in 1900 knew little about the lives their husbands led. While she saw such sheltered existence as stultifying, she nevertheless recognized that when women did gain worldly understanding, they had no power to change whatever they found amiss. Only painful disillusionment and resigned acceptance result from enlightenment, as in "The Lamp of Psyche" (1895),[8] when a woman learns that her husband had avoided military service by questionable means, and in "The Letters" (1910), when a woman discovers unopened all the love letters she had written her husband before their marriage. In both stories, ironic endings suggest that the husbands never even notice that the adoration of their wives has turned to patient forbearance.

Wharton's humorous approach to divorce in "The Other Two" (1904) was remarkable for its time. Despite its light tone, it raised questions about the benefits and dangers of the growing incidence of divorce and remarriage as these are reflected from the point of view of Alice's third husband, Waythorn. At the close of the story, he takes the third cup of tea—after the other two men are served—and does so with a laugh. But the reader is aware of his ambivalence toward his new marriage, toward his wife who accommodates easily to all three men, and toward himself as a man who feels himself superior to the other two and possibly to Alice and may be embarrassed about such feelings. Perhaps the sense of possession, intimacy, and privacy cannot be attained in a marriage to a partner who has shared her love and life too completely with others.

Wharton suggests varying answers to the question of the degree of choice that remains to a woman after marriage in three of her astringent tales: "Fullness of Life" (1891), "The Reckoning" (1904), and "The Quicksand" (1904). In "Souls Belated" (1899) she implies that marriage may be an artificial formality and a mere extraneous convention when love invests a liaison outside of marriage, but that compromise with conventions may undergird love more satisfactorily than the troublesome seeking of freedom from conventions. She was still wrestling with such problems almost three decades later in *The Children* and *The Gods Arrive,* indicating that the personal, psychological, and sexual problems confronting women at the turn of the century were not to be resolved in her lifetime. Later excellent stories centering on these themes, which R. W. B. Lewis designates "The Marriage Question,"[9] include "Autres Temps," "The Day of the Funeral," "Joy in the House," "Diagnosis," "Roman Fever," and "Pomegranate Seed." Wharton's final story, "All Souls," presents a woman who has had a satisfying marriage that has left her with the confidence to live alone and the wish to do so in the home that she and her husband enjoyed. Nevertheless, she finds herself vulnerable to fear and less able to cope independently without her husband than she had expected. "Roman Fever," "Pomegranate Seed," and "All Souls" hold special significance in Wharton's work because they are sure evidence that she retained the ability to write good fiction to the end of her life.

The "projection of . . . inner consciousness"

Wharton reveals remarkable subtlety in "The Eyes" (1910), an acute analysis of the blindness of the aesthetic temperament. She is concerned in this tale with the ramifications of Andrew Culwin's moral deficiencies as they have undermined his own life and the lives of others. A gracious, wealthy, cultured man, Culwin surrounds himself with disciples. Twice, at times of self-satisfaction, when he has judged that he has acted in a kindly way, he has had a vision of leering red eyes at night. Whether they are the result of faulty vision, hallucination, or "a projection of my inner consciousness," the reader alone must decide. A master at self-deception, Culwin cannot see, until the final moment in the story, that the eyes are a symbol of his own hidden weakness. Irony derives from his assurance, before he relates his experience to his disciples, that he is done now and forever with the apparition, whereas he himself becomes the apparition.

At the completion of the tale, he is amused when one of the young men recoils from him. At last, as he looks into the mirror, he recognizes the lurid countenance with its horrible eyes as his own. The supernatural has, in fact, become the natural; the fearful hallucination has become the even more terrifying actuality and emphasizes the completeness of Culwin's degeneration. In contrast to James's more discursive supernatural narratives, Wharton often made use of a single obsessive and obtrusive image to organize a given tale. The lurid eyes are, furthermore, a compelling projection of the slightly decadent atmosphere surrounding Culwin even in his beautiful library and of his moral occlusion: his inability to realize that complacent noninvolvement in human relationships represents, in reality, the most despicable kind of involvement.

In "Bewitched" (1926) Wharton analyzes psychic reactions and uses supernatural phenomena symbolically in studying the effects of isolation and fear in a remote New England locale. Prudence Rutledge alleges that her husband, Saul, has for a year been bewitched and gradually debilitated by the ghost of a girl, Ora Brand, in whom he had been interested before his marriage. With quiet malignity, Mrs. Rutledge insists that a stake—undoubtedly a phallic emblem—be driven through the breast of the dead girl to keep her ghost from walking and to release Saul from the spell that is compelling him to meet her spirit. Mrs. Rutledge almost certainly thinks of her as a succubus who must afford Saul an intense, if illicit, sexual satisfaction that contrasts with Prudence Rutledge's frigidity.

Prudence summons three neighbors to carry out her demand, one o whom is Sylvester Brand, the widowed father of the "witch"; another, Orri Bosworth, the recording consciousness of the story; and the third, Deaco Hibben a local ecclesiastic. That evening the men discover a woman's foo prints in the snow leading from the cemetery to the hut, which has been th trysting place. One of them fires a shot, and something white rises up in th darkness. A few days later, Brand's other daughter, Venny, dies of pneumo nia, and Bosworth suspects that Ora has drawn her sister to the grave in he loneliness, now that her lover has eluded her spell. Ambiguity enough r mains for us to suppose that Venny may have been the "ghost," but we ide tify too strongly with the sensible Bosworth to accept absolutely a detach and rational explanation. The characters seldom lose control of themselv the action is underplayed, and their control of their inner distress enables us identify closely with them.

The effectiveness of the tale derives mostly from Mrs. Rutledge and fron the imaginative intensity with which Wharton envisioned her; the spectacle of the sinner and his or her punishment animates Mrs. Rutledge. For a woman who believes so compulsively the precept on her parlor wall, "The Soul that Sinneth It Shall Die," it is but a step to proclaim, "Thou shalt not suffer a witch to live." In her obsession with the vanquishing of evil, Prudence reveals her own blindness to mercy, faith, and compassion. She is a blighting presence, as the references to her marblelike pallor, her white eyelids, her cold eyes "like sightless orbs" or "marble eye-balls," and her shriveled hands indicate. Relaxed after the funeral of Venny, she remarks casually, "it sometimes seems as if we were all waking right in the Shadow of Death."

The narrator of the tale, Bosworth, provides its other chief focus, and its complexities of meaning are mostly developed through his reflections upon character and incident. Through him, Wharton maintains the single point of view at the same time that she juxtaposes his varying depths of consciousness to achieve intense dramatic effect. Like the narrator in *Ethan Frome*, Bosworth is less provincial than the people he describes; unlike him, Bosworth is basically a Hemlock County man, whose feelings—in spite of his intellectual reservations—are rooted in generations of belief in witches and ghosts.

The effectiveness of this story results from Wharton's understanding of the difficulties to be endured in New England rural life. The stoical withstanding of hardship is a measure of the strength of the characters, but their isolation makes them prey to neurotic fears. Sylvester Brand is an alienated man with the laugh of one who has never known gaiety. He works hard to no purpose on his barren land. His wife and both daughters die young. At the funeral of Venny, his face suggests that he is now going home alone, identified only with death: "Brand's face was the closed door of a vault, barred with wrinkles like bands of iron." It is no accident that the story—like another ominous tale, "The Triumph of Night," and like *Ethan Frome*—takes place in the depth of the New England winter when the physical landscape can reinforce the psychic tensions oppressing the people in the community. There is no sharp line between the normal and the abnormal psyche nor between the real and the supernatural. In the vast, remote area, covered by snow, the sharp line between psychic dislocation and the spirit world dissolves.

In symbolic power and psychological subtlety, "After Holbein" (1928) presents another culmination in Wharton's mastery of the short story form. The decadence of an old aristocracy and the peculiar perspective on life available to those approaching death provide its themes; and the Holbein woodcuts of *The Dance of Death* provide its inspiration. The protagonist, Anson Warley, is a bachelor dilettante who is also an Everyman figure, confronted as all must finally be by death. Irony suffuses his situation and generates pathos for us as he realizes too late that he has wasted his life in incessant social pursuits in a shallow society.

As a young man, Anson Warley had embraced standards of excellence. Evelina Jaspar, once the leading hostess of New York society, is now senile; but she refuses to relinquish her role in it. Almost daily she plans parties, checks guest lists, dresses in velvet gown and jewels, dons a purplish wig, and greets imaginary guests. Her situation supplies an antiphonal comment on Warley's; and his, in turn, refracts and defines hers. Though Warley is ill for several hours with ominous symptoms of an impending stroke, he finds his way to her doorstep in formal dress. Their diminished activities this night, in effect, caricature what had formerly been merely a caricature of life as they participate again in the social activities of a deadened society with its gracious rituals and irresponsible attitudes.

Death pervades the entire story, which covers one day, includes many flashbacks to the earlier lives of the two, and culminates in the banquet scene. Just as the skeleton in the Holbein engravings summons his figures to death, Anson and Evelina are such spiritual skeletons to each other. Each is the other's victim, perhaps, but each is also the agent who brings the other to a confrontation of a final, inescapable reality. Because of their infirmities, which make them perceptive at some points and unexpectedly oblivious to reality at others, a confused dreamlike or "ghostly" atmosphere invests the story. Strange perspectives and patterns appear, as when Anson in the forenoon suffers a dizzy spell and sees the universe from a new angle as he recovers. In the final scene, imaginary guests file into Evelina's dining room; and, after this "ghostly cortège" has passed, Evelina and Anson "advance with rigid smiles and eyes straight ahead." They recognize the nonmaterial people sitting with them at the table, and they see food and flowers not visible to the nurse and maid observing the scene "off-stage." In a parody of the Last Supper, the vintage wine is soda water, and the bread is unsavory mashed potatoes. Yet a kind of fellowship is reached, a moment of spiritual communication long absent in their lives.

Tragedy lies not in the death of the principals, since death is a fate no one evades, but in the pointless lives they have led. Excessive sympathy for the characters would have weakened the Faustian inevitability of this final scene: Anson has lost the "Alps and the cathedrals" he had once dreamed of, but he and Evelina have had the sterile satisfactions that they settled for. They have paid for their death-in-life with the death of their own souls. Both have made life itself a dance of death. "After Holbein" is a parable that signifies that the wages of wasted talent are death and that complacency may indeed be the greatest of social sins.

Wharton used a wide variety of psychic phenomena in her stories of terror, including the evocation of ghosts, the uncertainty of memory, the occurrence of the demonic or the uncanny, the mystery of spirit-possession, and the distortions of time and nature as one finds them in a dream. Through these means, she provided unusual angles of penetration and a new perspective from which to view the strange or unfamiliar in human experience as it impinges on the mundane. She used psychic phenomena symbolically, and saw no need to document exactly the supernatural occurrence, preferring to hover between the worlds of the natural and the supernatural. Ambiguity characterizes the situations and tone of her best stories, particularly their endings. Consequently, the effect lingers as the reader ponders the tale long after it has been told.

In her later stories, Wharton establishes such ambiguities even more effectively, as in "Pomegranate Seed" and "All Souls." In "Pomegranate Seed" she introduces the ordinary routines of home life and marriage to establish a substratum for the action. When Kenneth Ashby marries Charlotte, he is careful, for one thing, to remove his dead wife's picture to the children's playroom. Over several months, however, the mysterious appearance in the mail at nine separate times of a gray envelope addressed in pale ink destroys the harmony of Kenneth's present marriage. Each time a letter appears, he becomes disturbed, leaves the room, and refuses to discuss it or to let his wife, Charlotte, read it. Charlotte decides that a beautiful home is not enough for them and that travel might reestablish harmony between herself and her husband. The morning Kenneth agrees to book passage for their journey, he disappears. Rushing to her mother-in-law for reassurance, Charlotte is lost in despair after the older woman recognizes the handwriting on the envelopes as that of Kenneth's domineering dead wife, Elsie. So shocked is she by the sight that she cannot even speak the name but communicates the identity of the writer to Charlotte simply by gazing fixedly at the wall where Elsie's picture had formerly hung. The material nature of the letters and the recognized penmanship validate the power of an actual ghost in this tale, although Charlotte's jealousy and lack of trust and Kenneth's inability to talk about his problems would adequately account for his leaving home.

In Wharton's late ghost stories the emphasis generally shifts to problems of relationships that are illuminated by some suggestion of a supernatural or extraordinary psychic experience. The difficult situations faced by characters in these stories can seldom be completely changed or the problems resolved, but the confrontation of the strange occurrence not only brings fear but forces an exploration of common human experience. Death and aging are recognized as inevitable, but Wharton explores other issues such as the need for spiritual sensitivity; the longing for independence; the crucial concern for others, or the lack of it; the misuse of power by the strong over the powerless; the juxtaposition of gossip, superstition, or custom with accurate historical information; the breakdown of communication, particularly among family members; and the temptation to live in a serene past rather than to face a disturbing present. Perhaps the most common theme running through Wharton's late ghost stories is her warning not to forfeit the sanctity of the soul through worship of the past, through nostalgia for a vanished society, or through grief for those who have died. Wharton recognized the temptation to look toward the past and to relinquish too easily the rewards that life may still offer. Stories developing this central theme include "After Holbein," "Kerfol," "Mr. Jones," "Pomegranate Seed," "The Looking Glass," and "All Souls."

In several of Wharton's ghost stories, a character is lured or forced away to a land of the dead—if not actually to death—through the influence of the ghost of a person from the past. In "Mr. Jones," a housekeeper exists in a state of nervous submission and finally dies because she has succumbed to the power of an already dead tyrant whose purpose had always been to imprison and dominate her, whereas a woman who challenges his mythic power by reading historical documents survives. In "Bewitched," Saul Rutledge is lured into a torpid, deathlike state, at first through fixation on a dead girl and the compelling memories of a lost love to which he tenaciously clings. In "Pomegranate Seed," Kenneth Ashby is lured away from his ongoing life with his new wife and children (and supposedly to death) because he hears in letters from his dead wife—letters illegible to others—the voice upon whose strength he had too completely depended. In "After Holbein," the senile Evelina Jasper and Anson Warley dance toward their own deaths in their ritual reversion to an already vanished aristocratic New York society.

Our understanding of Edith Wharton as a mature artist and as an older human being is enlarged by study of her late ghost stories, particularly when we consider them in relation to her autobiography, her finished and unfinished novels, and her other late stories. Her dedication of *Ghosts* (published just after her death) to Walter de la Mare leaves unanswerable questions. We can discover no record of his knowing Wharton, nor of his response to the dedication. We cannot be sure of the reasons for her attraction to his work—particularly his "ghostly" fiction—nor can we be sure of his influence upon her own stories. Nevertheless, it is clear that she saw in him a kindred soul and that the relationships between the stories of the supernatural and terror by these two authors enrich the reading of all of Wharton's late work.

In their ambiguous suggestion of the supernatural in the context of the natural, both Wharton and de la Mare create the eerie through an emphasis upon silence, suffocation, emptiness, or solitude. Wharton comes closest to de la Mare's dreamy, hypnotic style in "A Bottle of Perrier" as she presents Medford's state of mind in his five days at the desert compound, where he languidly accepts inactivity, isolation, and intense heat until an uneasy restlessness imperceptibly grows into an overwhelming fear.

In their stories both Wharton and de la Mare impressively relate silence to fear, although occasionally silence symbolizes peace. Characters are struck dumb after seeing an apparition; ghosts are often unable to make a sound; people fear that ghosts may be listening to them in the silence enveloping them; and silence may even become palpable—something one can touch or that weighs one down or smothers a victim. The two writers intensify the effects of silence by the use of natural conditions, such as fog, snow, soft wind, intense heat, or paralyzing cold. Both authors dramatically communicate the sense of a silence so absolute and unending that some of their stories suggest an atmosphere of total emptiness, impenetrable solitude, and exposure of the infinite—in fact, the presence of death in life. Except for "All Souls," Wharton's "Kerfol" may be her best story pervaded notably by silence. As the narrator arrives at the walled estate, he is impressed by the majesty of Kerfol, but feels it has the atmosphere of a great tomb. He finds himself oddly overcome by a longing for silence: "I wanted only to sit there and be penetrated by the weight of its silence." He is encircled by mute and sad-faced dogs, but only the eyes, not the voices, of the animals express their suffering, and he gradually realizes that these are the ghosts of dogs killed by a man of great cruelty centuries before and that they are the ghostly reminders of the silent past only whispered among the villagers as they are said to appear once each year.

De la Mare's best story dependent on silence is the gripping tale "All Hallows," which resembles "All Souls" in its prolonged tension as the narrator gropes in total darkness and inexplicable fear. The narrator (a pilgrim), who has walked for miles on an extremely hot day, and an elderly verger move slowly and fearfully through a huge and ancient church in total darkness and silence, guided only by a single candle. They believe that strongly purposive and malignant ghosts inhabit the church, All Hallows, which overlooks the ocean. It is as if these visitors to the church are lost in time as well as in the darkness and silence.

Similarly, silence pervades Wharton's last story, "All Souls." On All Souls'

Eve, the day when religious people honor their dead and when the supersti-
tious say ghosts leave their graves, Sara Clayburn's life becomes a haunted
one. Silence for the next thirty-six hours makes more oppressive Sara's abandonment in her country house by her servants, even those who have been
with her many years. She has been helpless in bed with a possibly broken
ankle, the maid's bell and the telephone are dead, the house has grown cold,
and the snow has filled the gutters and wrapped the house in a tomblike silence. After hours of waiting for a servant to come to her, she drags herself
inch by inch through her large empty house and hours later in this agonizing
journey yields to a fear of something that is not human.

Wharton communicates with skill and power the sense of absolute and
unending silence, suggesting a total emptiness, an impenetrable isolation, an
illimitable expanse as of the infinite. The cold house seems to Sara Clayburn
to have become a sepulcher: "It chilled her to feel there was no limit to this silence, no outer margin, nothing beyond it." Silence envelops her. "There was
no break, no thinnest crack in it anywhere . . . it was folded down on her like
a pall. She was sure that the nearness of any other human being, however
dumb and secret, would have made a faint crack in the texture of that silence,
flawed it as a sheet of glass is flawed by a pebble thrown against it." Wrapped
in this stifling shroud of silence, Sara Clayburn expects to die "of cold and the
terror of solitude." Throughout Sara's hours of delirium and panic, her
thoughts return to the unpleasant female stranger she had encountered near
her home as she returned from her walk at dusk, just before she injured her
ankle. She associates the stranger with the servants' heartless abandonment
of her and with her injury.

Sara Clayburn is, in part, the author's self-portrait. We know that Sara
was in her early fifties when her husband died, but we do not know her age at
the time of this story. She is a strong woman who loves her country home. Independent and self-assured, she is known to do the contrary of what people
advise—at least according to the unreliable narrator, her aggressive and insistent cousin. Sara is, in reality, a positive person with a "quick imperious nature," who vigorously tramps daily along the road. She knows everyone in the
area, and she efficiently keeps up her correspondence. Her servants have been
with her many years, and she feels a concern for their needs. All these characteristics of energy, discipline, composure, self-assertion, and concern for
neighbors and servants reflect Edith Wharton's own behavior for most of her
adult life. She has the whimsical imagination and the playful humor that
Wharton's friends say she possessed to the end of her life. Even when Sara becomes aware of the strange situation of her abandonment, she stubbornly re-

fuses to yield to fear for several hours. Ultimately, however, she expresses her trepidation in terms of approaching death and the "terror of solitude."

For a year after this unnerving episode, Sara seeks to become the confident and sensible woman she had been before. Then on All Souls' Eve, the anniversary of her trauma, she has a second encounter outside her door with the rude female stranger. Sara asserts herself and orders the woman to leave. The woman laughs insultingly but disappears into the fog before Sara's eyes. Sara flees to the city home of her cousin, as at the close of "Pomegranate Seed" Charlotte Ashby rushes to a motherly relative for reassurance and receives instead only further evidence that her fears are well-founded.

Wharton's ability to maintain an ambiguous tone regarding the "fetch" or "witch" is especially impressive in this last story, because the conflicting belief and disbelief concerning the fetch exist not in one mind but in two. Sara remains to the end of her life unsure about the supernatural nature of the malevolent force that twice entered her life on All Souls' Eve. Her cousin, who was not present but has read much on witchcraft, firmly believes that a fetch or witch will threaten Sara again if she returns home and that Sara's servants are somehow in league with devils.

Wharton never states that Sara Clayburn believes in witches or is susceptible to the excesses associated with the covens. Rather, she indicates a sharp contrast between Sara and her cousin in their approach to the supernatural. Sara long refuses to confide her fears to this garrulous cousin who avidly reads popular literature on witches and who finds the notion of covens titillating and Sara's situation arresting. She circulates rumors of Sara's bad weekend after the first appearance of the fetch and feels self-important in being able to inform Sara of the possibility that her best and oldest servant is a medium for the forces of evil.

Sara fears what, she insists, she does not believe in—an uncontrollable, undefinable force of evil. Her more immediate fears are abandonment, solitude, and death—the universally haunting realities of the independent individual. After the second appearance of the fetch makes Sara flee, the cousin immediately assumes the role of mother of a troubled infant, and Sara allows herself for the first time to be treated as a frightened child, undressed, and tucked into bed. Because Sara, the intelligent and vigorous woman, needs emotional support against a repetition of her disorganizing experience and her sense that she is helpless against superhuman forces, she must now return to the mothering care of this woman to whom she has never felt close, and she must again succumb to her childlike longing for comfort and warmth.

Much of the interest in the story derives from Wharton's skill in presenting two women who see life differently and who also interpret differently this ambiguous and mysterious situation. Sara reconciles herself to a dependent and silent life as she suddenly becomes an old woman, and she avoids acknowledgement of her psychological suffering. Her cousin, never silent, continues with relish to tell Sara's exciting and shocking story, embellished by her imagination.

Chapter Seven
The Late Novels: 1922–1928

Wharton's Career after 1920: A Refusal to Stop Growing

Edith Wharton's late works exhibit her continued ability to confront, with a varying degree of success, new and challenging social issues and artistic problems. In the 1920s and 1930s, she published a third of her short stories and *Old New York* (1924), which collected her last four novellas. During these late years she also wrote a volume of criticism, *The Writing of Fiction* (1925); her autobiography, *A Backward Glance* (1934); and numerous critical articles. But most important are her novels, seven of which show a sustained talent: *A Son at the Front* (1922), *The Mother's Recompense* (1925), *Twilight Sleep* (1927), *The Children* (1928), *Hudson River Bracketed* (1929), *The Gods Arrive* (1932), and *The Buccaneers* (1938). Another novel, *Glimpses of the Moon* (1922), though poorly received by most critics, nevertheless became a best-seller and was made into a popular movie.

She had begun *A Son at the Front* before her greater success, *The Age of Innocence*. Unfortunately, the fact that she did not complete this war novel until 1922 colored its critical fortunes. It is a better book than most commentators have conceded it to be. In *Twilight Sleep* and *The Children* she was less restrained than she had previously been in writing the comedy of manners, and the objects of her satire were broader. She wrote mostly about the deficiencies and absurdities to be found in contemporary middle-class and upper-class families, with the result that there is little of the elegiac communication of a lost way of life that had been insistent in *The Age of Innocence*.

Hudson River Bracketed, which traces the life of an artist, though complete in itself, must be considered in relation to its sequel, *The Gods Arrive*. In both books Wharton analyzed the problems that an artist must face in a materialistic and philistine society, and the typical sexual choices he must make to find emotional fulfillment in marriage or outside it. In her unfinished novel, *The Buccaneers,* she returned to the New York past that had always haunted her imagination but about which she had not written in a novel since *The Age of Innocence*. The substantial fragment reveals not only a high level of artistry but an Edith Wharton in a more hopeful mood than is to be discerned in most of her other late works.

Wharton experimented in her late career with a variety of contemporary characters and situations; and she extended her comic and satiric range to the use of overstatement and flamboyant mockery even beyond that found in *The Custom of the Country* and her most stylized short stories. To the end, she reflected in her fiction a vigorous interest in contemporary American life, which she saw with incisiveness and sympathy. Until her death, she continued to write about the themes that had already absorbed her: the artist's relationship to the marketplace; the relation of a man's art to his personal life; the effect upon the individual of changing attitudes toward marriage, sex, and divorce; the centrifugal effects of the modern economy on the family; and—in her ghost stories—the shadowy relationship between the psychological and the supernatural.

But Wharton's new concerns were also evident in these late works when she wrote sympathetically, yet critically, about the alienation and frustration of men and women in an impersonalized and rootless postwar era. Her concern with the isolation of people in all age groups—with the gulf in understanding between generations, and with the relations between parents and children—became more insistent. She developed an overriding interest in the relationship of her characters to a shapeless social milieu. The "tribal ceremonies" of the old New Yorkers in *The Age of Innocence* could no longer give form to the lives of those in the postwar era. Banal substitutes for the lost values emerged in the exaggerated involvement of her characters with committees, ladies' culture clubs, religious cults, and bohemian gatherings of artists at certain cafés. Unfortunately, the causes espoused by these groups are often meaningless enterprises at best and fraudulent schemes at worst, and superficial involvement in them simply disguises the basic aimlessness of those who participate. If marital loyalties imprisoned a responsible person for life in *The Age of Innocence*, divorce and free love do not liberate so much as complicate lives in the later books as ex-spouses and stepparents multiply. More than ever, Wharton emphasized the need for sharpened awareness in her personae, but, ironically, the pressures of the age deadened sensibility instead of enlarging it.

The author rated her late fiction more highly than did some critics, who found in it inadequate technical resources, an uninteresting version of experience, and an inability to reflect with accuracy the conditions of contemporary life. When in 1936 she named her favorite works, she included, in addition to *The Custom of the Country* and *Summer,* her most recent novels, *The Children, Hudson River Bracketed,* and *The Gods Arrive.*[1] Although none of the added novels is a masterpiece, the new directions that she explored in them gave them stature, interest, importance, and some degree of influence.

Study of Wharton's fiction after 1920 has only begun to correct such misconceptions about her late career as that she had lost her artistic skill, that she had lost touch with the modern world, that she no longer understood America, and that she did not understand the younger generation. In all her late novels, except *The Buccaneers,* she used the contemporary scene; in all, she created some sympathetic youthful characters; and in all, she confronted, through her central figures, the problems arising from the conflicts between generations. Even though *The Buccaneers* is laid in an earlier time, it presents social change positively—with hope, humor, and enthusiasm.

The Realist's Reaffirmation: "plunging both hands into the motley welter"

Although Wharton was not enthusiastic about some new trends in writing and in literary criticism in her later life, she nevertheless continued to be interested in contemporary literature and to feel an affinity for certain younger writers. In *The Writing of Fiction,* her aim, she said, was to help new writers—not to defend her own views on literature. She wrote graciously in 1925 to F. Scott Fitzgerald after he had sent her a copy of *The Great Gatsby* with a friendly dedication, and she told him that his gesture had touched her and that she would send her latest book to him in return, "in a spirit of sincere deprecation." She assured him that in his novel he had taken a great leap beyond his earlier work; and she took time to praise several separate scenes and characters that "augur still greater things."[2] Sinclair Lewis acknowledged her as an inspiration and model for his work by dedicating *Babbitt* to her in 1922.

In the later years of her life Wharton maintained a surprising number of contacts with young Americans. With these young people, Wharton's shyness vanished; and she enabled them to overcome any shyness in approaching her. Percy Lubbock described the encounters as "fun" for both her and her guests: "There was a quick light of amusement and understanding, as though she knew where she was . . . needing no introduction . . . all was well, and they could talk—and talk they must. . . . A delightful sight, and always delightful because there was no false touch in it whatever—none of patronage, none of condescension, none of benevolent superiority, least of all of any strain for an effect. She was equal in the fun."[3]

Wharton's views on literature set her apart from the literary trends gaining prominence in the 1920s and 1930s, sometimes, it must be admitted, to the detriment of her work. She did not endorse such innovations in technique and subject matter as stream of consciousness, which she associated with the imitators of James Joyce, or the explicit treatment of sex, which in her view disregarded subtleties and sensitivity and which she associated with D. H. Lawrence and James Joyce. She also rejected the use of some naturalistic or slice-of-life techniques, which often, in the interest of presenting a reportorial kind of social actuality, stripped man of his dignity as a human being and revealed him simply as a passive victim of deterministic forces. Also uncongenial to her was the sociologically oriented fiction that became a hallmark of the Great Depression. She recognized, however, the need to adapt conventional methods to suggest in fiction the turbulence and spiritual malaise of modern society; and, to some extent, she responded in her novels of the 1920s and 1930s by employing a more rapid shifting of scene and point of view and by treating social, intellectual, and sexual issues more explicitly. But she continued to emphasize firmly, as the keystone of fiction, the need for selection of detail, for an ordered and sequential structure, and for definiteness and progression in the revelation of characters.

Writers, she thought, should check any tendency to react negatively to the accelerating changes in society after the war. Instead, they must recognize that any attempt to deny the realities of the life that surrounded them would be stultifying, ultimately, to their art. For better or for worse, they must work with the society of which they are a part, even when they find their milieu distasteful. In 1927, in "The Great American Novel," she defined writers' responsibility as she saw it and urged them to come to terms with the new society that had emerged from the war. For her, this society was "ephemeral, shifting, but infinitely curious to study"; and American writers, she thought, had largely passed it by in their hurry to experiment and to assimilate such modern thinkers as Freud and Marx: "It is useless, at least for the story teller, to deplore what the new order of things has wiped out, vain to shudder at what it is creating; there it is, whether for better or worse, and the American novelist . . . can best use his opportunity by plunging both hands into the motley welter."[4] So spoke Edith Wharton, who was the artist and the realist to the end of her life.

A Son at the Front

A Son at the Front (1922) rises above Wharton's other writings about the war in its candor—in her recognition in particular that selfishness tempers most patriotism. The novel is not concerned with heroism on the battlefield so much as with the conflict between courage and fear, whether justifiable or not, experienced by those on the home front. Wharton scrutinizes, on the one hand, the parents' selfish and narrow lives; on the other, their grief and bereavements, which they face with endurance, if not always with dignity.

The "son at the front" is George Campton, whose artist-father, John Campton, and whose mother and stepfather, Julia and Anderson Brant, are wealthy American expatriates living in France. John Campton, a successful American artist who has lived long in Paris, has owed, at least in his view, part of his success to the freedom that accrued to him when he secured a divorce from his wife, Julia. Wife and child, he had assumed, could only burden him and prevent his personal and artistic development. He has recently developed, however, a strong attachment to his son, George—an attachment that suggests feelings of guilt about his long neglect. When George's mother became the wife of Anderson Brant, a wealthy Parisian banker, Brant became attached to him and cared for him in childhood and adolescence.

Wharton sympathetically presents the activities of all three parents as they diligently try, throughout the early part of the novel, to keep George from being conscripted and then from being sent to the front. His own decision to volunteer for service at the battlefront is apparently the result of an impulse, and his decision baffles the reader as much as it does his parents in that his mood and his personality, as Wharton has presented them early in the book, do not provide the motivation for such radical action. Heretofore, his patriotism had been low-key, to say the least.

Actually, George figures in few scenes in the book; he is talked about more than he is seen. He refuses to continue his relationship with his longtime mistress after she indicates her unwillingness to divorce her husband to marry him. Again, the motivation for George's action is baffling to his mistress and to his father, stepfather, and mother; and the motivation in terms of his function in the novel is again nebulous. George somehow thinks it more responsible to leave his beloved a widow, should he die at the front. He is wounded, recovers, returns to the front, and is killed; but his tale is not at an end. It continues with the grief of his relatives and with the relief they all feel when the Americans finally arrive to avenge not only the outrages perpetrated upon France but the death of the young man they have all loved.

Wharton's undisguised, chauvinistic pro-French, anti-German bias and the depression her characters feel in response to America's delayed entry into the conflict tend to limit the universality of the novel. In simply dismissing this book, however, along with the other books she produced on the war (*Fighting France*, 1915; *The Book of the Homeless*, 1916; *The Marne*, 1918; and *French Ways and Their Meaning*, 1919), critics have overlooked

Wharton's satiric aplomb in this novel and her genuine creative involvement with her subject. In *A Son at the Front,* her satire constantly relates to the main action of the book and establishes its mordant, sardonic tone. Previously, in both *The Marne* and *Fighting France,* Wharton had briefly chided flamboyant patriots who enjoyed the drama of the war—those whose patriotism had to be "fed on pictures of little girls singing the Marseillaise in Alsatian headdresses and old men with operatic waistcoats tottering forward to kiss the flag."[5] This line of attack is developed further in *A Son at the Front,* where she criticizes the self-serving motives of many of her bored and restless characters who find fulfillment for their empty natures only through the war. In this period, Wharton's short stories and her *Twilight Sleep* are also critical of those Americans who pursue aimless lives, align themselves insincerely with various causes, or devote themselves to passing enthusiasms. The touch of cynicism that links *A Son at the Front* to the satires that follow it not only lends distinction to the book but also lifts it beyond sentimentality and propaganda.

Wharton is always sensitive in her presentation of wartime French society to the subtle hypocrisy underlying the behavior of those at home. After George is sent to the front, Julia Brant takes pleasure in the phrase, "my son at the front," but she finds her role as mother of a potential hero unnatural. In a storm of activity, she stages public bridge parties in her mansion to raise money for war relief, and she surrenders her drawing room to lectures about German atrocities. In an effective satiric scene, Harvey Mayhew, an American delegate to The Hague who was appalled during a brief detention in a German jail at being accosted by prostitutes, lectures in Mrs. Brant's drawing room to the accompaniment of stirring martial music. When he is interrupted by the receipt of a telegram informing him that his nephew is missing in action, he collapses, and reality forcibly erases the sham. He has enjoyed rallying war enthusiasm, but he cannot face the cost of war to himself as an individual. In the same scene, Wharton sternly satirizes those parents who openly grieve with a bereaved individual while they secretly rejoice that they themselves have been spared such news for one more day.

In this novel Wharton engenders such intensity of atmosphere and utilizes such an extensive range of incisive detail that she gradually conveys the impression of a world completely dedicated to war. The immediacy of the mobilization, the fund-raising rallies, and the efforts to draw America into the war become stirring realities even while Wharton continues her paced narrative of events. The characters, no matter how frivolous or superficial, cannot evade the agony that results from the war when personal loss is all but universal. The totality of such suffering is overwhelming; and, to her credit as artist,

Wharton consummately re-creates the tragic impact of a worldwide cataclysm as it affects a group of people whose affluence and social prestige has
previously protected them from the unpleasant and the violent. In her novel,
people suffer so much that they can see nothing beyond war and nothing un-
related to war. She communicates the magnitude of the debacle by multiply-
ing incidents for a cumulative effect: telegrams arrive with every post to
announce another casualty until it seems as if everyone must have received at
least one. In producing this pervasive sense of a world convulsed by war, of a
world driven apart by the opportunism of the few and the grief of the many,
Wharton gives the book a timeless significance.

In this impressive panorama of all-encompassing war, she unfortunately
minimizes its differing psychological impact on her characters. They are not
fully developed as individuals; their fates are challenging simply because
these people happen to live in a time of crisis. But the novel fails to achieve
the highest excellence because Wharton fails to objectify her characters—to
make them more important than the milieu against which they are posed.
Her artistry moves us to grieve for all who die and for all who mourn, but we
seldom know who these people are as we do those in her other novels.

A profusion of potentially strong characters promises amplitude for the
novel, but they drift away before they can make any durable impression.
Adele Anthony comes to Paris to help her alcoholic brother become a sculptor. She stays there for another generation after her brother is "shipped
home," but she functions only as a confidante for George and John Campton
and as one more volunteer for charitable work. Madge Talkett, George's mistress, disappointingly fades out of the novel. All the characters who touch the
artist's life become noteworthy not for their relationship to him but for their
relationship to the war. Failing to become sharply defined persons, they re-
cede into the background. However, this muting of the personal may have
been by design, because war allows no individual to be important. The war
dwarfs the characters to the detriment of *A Son at the Front* as a psychological
testament but to its advantage as a remarkable re-creation of a world that has
lost its moorings.

Wharton succeeds to some extent in developing the relationships between
George Campton and his artist-father, his stepfather, and his mother. She
does not, however, adequately exploit either the complicated relationship between John Campton, the father, and Anderson Brant, the stepfather, or their
rivalry for the possession of George's affections. John Campton mourns the
years that he has missed in his son's life by deserting his family, but he tends
irrationally to blame Brant rather than himself for this situation. He domi-
neers over the self-deprecatory Anderson Brant as if to prove that the artist

surpasses the businessman and that the father outranks the stepfather. The situation of the two men is close and filled with dramatic tension that they can seldom express; it is a highly suggestive situation even if it is not explored to the depth we ordinarily expect in Wharton's work.

John Campton must humble himself to enlist Brant's aid in getting George assigned to a safe job in the army; and the two men must, in enforced intimacy, travel together in Brant's fine automobile to the front lines where George lies severely wounded in a field hospital. Later, they try together to understand George's secret love affair with Madge Talkett. Finally, several months after George's death, John Campton manages to overcome his resentment of Brant and his money to the extent of consenting to fashion a monument for George's grave from marble paid for by the stepfather, who is grieving as desperately as he for the same son lost at the front.

That the two parents, mourning inconsolably, are the father and the stepfather—rather than the estranged father and mother joined in grief—adds a memorable psychological dimension to the novel; but it is an aspect that Wharton does not fully analyze. Julia Brant appears after George's death only as Campton thinks back on the funeral. He remembers being struck with the "perversity of attention" when he finds himself thinking about Julia's blue-red, unpowdered nose under her heavy veil at the funeral, instead of about the coffin, draped with flags and flanked by glittering candles, which seems remote from him though it is only a few feet away. He pities Julia more than he does anyone else, seeing her as an "empty-hearted old woman" who will feel more isolated when she realizes how much more Brant loved George than she did and how much more he is suffering from his death. Curiously, Campton pities his former wife because he knows she will now have to fill her life with more bridge parties while her husband is occupied with his grief for her son.

A Son at the Front deserves more recognition than Frederick J. Hoffman, for example, accorded it when he lumped it with the fiction that Dorothy Canfield Fisher and Willa Cather wrote about the war.[6] He viewed *A Son at the Front,* like Fisher's *The Deepening Stream* (1930) and Cather's *One of Ours* (1922), as a novel by an older-generation woman who could not, as a noncombatant, know the war firsthand as younger participants in it, such as Ernest Hemingway and John Dos Passos, could. *A Son at the Front* is not a battlefield novel, however; it is a novel depicting the social stresses and strains that the war entailed among the civilian populace as a whole. The novel is authentic enough; and it stemmed from the author's firsthand experience as a wartime administrator. Outrage, which finds its vent in satire, and sympathy, which finds its expression in compassion, determined the quality of Wharton's by-no-means-negligible war novel.

The Mother's Recompense

In a 1902 fragment titled "Disintegration," Wharton began a novel about the unhappy Clephane family, and she continually returned to it. In the fragment Wharton emphasized the loneliness of the incompatible couple's small daughter; in the 1925 novel *The Mother's Recompense*, she summarized in a few paragraphs Kate Clephane's memories of eighteen years—her unhappy marriage, her escape, her abandonment by the man who assisted in the escape, her punishment by relatives upon her return after two years, her futile attempts to see her daughter, her exile to the Riviera with only a small income, her feeling of being reborn in a brief affair, her abandonment by this lover, her recognition for relief work during the war, and her seemingly pointless routine of teas, committee meetings, fund raising for her church, and shopping. Her previous life in the United States and the people connected with that distant past are now almost unreal to her.

In the finished novel Wharton changed the focus of her book from the child, Anne, the central figure in the 1902 version, to the mother. Kate is presented as an imperfect woman but as one who is determined to get all she can from life. The presentation of Kate, largely from her own viewpoint, is relatively sympathetic rather than strongly judgmental. For some readers, this tolerance of an impulsive woman and her muddled life allows the novel to succeed; for others, the themes of moral choice become too confused and the problems of using Kate's point of view limit the integrity and the aesthetic effect of the book. Although *The Custom of the Country* was criticized for the harshness of its satire, this mildly satirical novel has been seen negatively for its failure to attack, rather than simply to recognize, the weaknesses of its main character.

Wharton's creation of Kate as a woman of considerable vulnerability and considerable persistence constitutes her greatest achievement in *The Mother's Recompense*. Even in the first pages of the book Kate reveals human—and representative—weaknesses, inconsistencies, and idiosyncrasies. She laughs, cries, and becomes fearful all in a matter of moments. She hates discovering that she is aging, but a few hours later she is tripping along the street singing to herself as she sets out to exchange new clothes designed to make her look young for more sedate but smart apparel. Her daughter's letter has inspired her to claim by her appearance that she is indeed a proud mother of a grown daughter.

Pretty, impulsive, and self-deprecating, she wakes that morning shocked that "after having been thirty-nine for a number of years she had suddenly become forty-four." She then engages in a comical conversation with herself, trying to figure out exactly how old her daughter now is and how old her cherished former lover, Chris Fenno, would be. In all candor, she admits that he was, and always will be, eleven years younger than she. Mathematics of this sort overwhelms her, and she drowsily feels blessed to have her one luxury—a maid to bring her hot chocolate. But Kate is too energetic to stay moody for long. Once her day has begun, her feelings and thoughts move like great waves, and these thoughts are as golden as the sun shining through the dust that rises up around her as she moves briskly along the street.

As soon as her daughter, Anne, telegraphs asking Kate to come live with her, she leaves for America. The major complication of the plot occurs when she learns that Chris Fenno and Anne are engaged. Since he left Kate, he has been decorated in the war and is now working as a journalist, rather than pursuing his painting. There are hints that he may have changed for the better, although the main change Kate notes is his "stoutness."

She tries to keep Chris and Anne apart, but recognizes that she is threatening her newfound relationship with her daughter in doing so. Faced with the dilemma of telling Anne that Chris is a dilettante and had once been her own lover, Kate wrestles with such complex moral issues as the value of honesty, the importance of a married or engaged person knowing the full truth about his or her betrothed, and the individual's need for freedom of choice in choosing a marital partner, as opposed to a parent's making that choice. Kate also struggles, perhaps even more painfully, with her own personal responses to the relationship. She would gladly have welcomed Chris back as her lover, if that had been possible. Kate, jealous because Chris prefers a much younger woman, may also feel some revulsion to the incestuous overtones of the situation. Wharton wrote to John Hugh Smith in 1925 that she felt the "full force" of the overtones of incest as she wrote *The Mother's Recompense* (*Letters*, 480).

The only solution that Kate sees to this situation is to abandon her long-lost daughter once more, in order to keep her secret from her forever. Wharton does not imply that one decision is better than another: morality is not simple, and compromises are a part of life; truth may be assumed to be better than deceit, but a full revelation of the past can destroy relationships among human beings—as she herself had illustrated in *The Reef* and *The Old Maid*. While a clergyman counsels Kate to tell the truth, he nevertheless suggests that she consider the possibility of keeping her secret rather than causing "sterile pain" for Anne. Kate leaves behind in America Chris Fenno, Anne, and Fred Landers (a friend for whom she had yearned for years but whom she now finds physically unattractive). The return to her mundane and lonely life in France is probably not tragic, for Kate has the consolation there of many women friends, divided into three groups, "frumps, hypocrites, and the 'good sort'—like herself." For Anne, the future may be more ominous because the truth has been withheld.

The critical response to this book was mixed at the time of its publication and remains so. The ending dissatisfies many readers as a sign of Kate's too apparent readiness to abandon her daughter a second time, now that Anne needs her. Kate's unconventional sexual behavior and attitudes disturbed early readers. Her dilemma about revealing Chris's true nature seems a bit factitious, because his worst behavior appears to have been his leaving Kate after a period of intimacy, as she herself had abandoned her husband and child much earlier. The title of the novel leads readers to expect that Kate will experience a specific punishment or reward as a result of her difficulties. That expectation is not fulfilled. The puzzled and often hostile reception of the book disturbed Wharton, as she reveals in a 9 June 1925 letter to Margaret Chanler: "You will wonder that the priestess of the Life of Reason shd [sic] take such things to heart; & I wonder too. I never have minded before; but as my work reaches its close, I feel so sure that it is either nothing, or far more than they know. . . . And I wonder, a little desolately, which?" (*Letters*, 483).

A Modern Comedy of Manners: *Twilight Sleep*

In *Twilight Sleep*, as in *The Children*, Wharton directed her satire toward restless Americans of the 1920s. She creates in these novels situations revealing the same understanding of the ways of the rich just before the crash of 1929 that characterized her earlier satires of the decadent aristocrats and newly rich of old New York. In both *Twilight Sleep* and *The Children*, individuals of integrity and potential find themselves caught in a dehumanizing milieu. Edmund Wilson, among the first to recognize Wharton's work written in a new satiric mode, viewed *Twilight Sleep* as an acute work of social criticism in which she had renewed her talent with the new age.[7] In this novel, he asserted, she interpreted the modern city with great intelligence. Actually, she was less involved with the city than with the modern family for whom wealth intensifies boredom and alienation. "Twilight sleep," the anesthesia used widely in the 1920s, especially in childbirth, symbolizes in the novel the attempts made by many in the postwar decade to escape reality, either through excessive and meaningless activity or through indolence and malaise.

Wharton adds perspective to the action by developing the novel through the consciousness of three different members of the same family, none of whom understands the other two. Adroitly, but pointedly, she shifts the point of view among the three: Nona Manford, a sensible and sensitive young woman, who serves as the author's voice; Pauline Manford, her mother, who is excessively efficient, strenuously interested in causes and cults, and distressed at her family's separation from her (although she expects her children to schedule appointments with her through her secretary); and Dexter Manford, who married Pauline hoping that she would read aloud to him in the evenings while he reviewed law cases in a corner of his mind. Instead, Dexter has found himself the victim of Pauline's perpetual campaign to keep him vigorous through involvement in social and cultural projects. He now discovers, moreover, that he is in love with Lita Wyant, the "flapper" wife of his stepson, Jim, who is a minor character but who is admirable in his love for his and Lita's child. Jim Wyant, is, in fact, a casualty of his selfish wife and of the society that countenances her and has produced her ennui. With comic perversity, Dexter daydreams of his ideal woman, who is far different from either Pauline or Lita. He fantasizes about a pioneer woman digging potatoes in Minnesota.

Wharton's secondary characters in this novel demonstrate her versatility in creating the flat characters who are effective in a stylized comedy of manners. Arthur Wyant, Pauline's ex-husband, is a gentle aristocrat who has become an alcoholic; Lita Wyant, who is bored with her husband and baby, plans to escape to Hollywood stardom; and Aggie Heuston, a lay nun, is the frigid wife of Stanley, the man whom Nona loves passionately and hopelessly. But, motivated by a stern puritanical code, Aggie refuses to divorce her husband, Stanley, because she sees passion as a danger from which she can "save" him. Her attempt to deny the importance of sex is just as much a form of "twilight sleep," in Wharton's view, as are Dexter's evasion of reality and his refusal to recognize his wife as a human being and his marriage as a human responsibility.

The disaster, toward which the whole novel builds, strikes at the Manford's elaborate country home when shots ring out after midnight; but the disaster is as much an illusion as the other aspects of the lives of these aristocrats. Pauline rushes into Lita's bedroom to discover that Arthur Wyant, in a dispute with Nona, has accidentally shot her. Nona had been trying to prevent him from killing her father, Dexter, who had been for some time with Lita in her bedroom during the absence of her husband, Jim. Fortunately, Nona suffers only a surface wound and retires a few weeks later to rural solitude to regain her emotional equilibrium.

The events after the shooting are sardonically comic and only incidentally tragic in their implications. In tragicomic confusion, the servants and the village fire department dramatically converge upon the bedroom. In the morning, the night of terror and humiliation has vanished like an hallucination induced by "twilight sleep." The participants hasten to deny the actualities of the situation and to present a doctored version of events to the public. These social leaders, incapable of facing the implications of what they have done, cannot inform the public of the truth. The butler has notified the police that a window was forced, and the morning papers accordingly report that a burglar fired the shots. The family members depart discreetly for Canada or Europe until they can return to New York with impunity, resume their careless lives where they have left them, and subject themselves again to the unrealities induced by "twilight sleep."

The principal critical point respecting this novel concerns the moral and aesthetic adequacy of this climactic shooting scene. Is it adequate for the novel? Is it an adequate expression of Wharton's satiric propensities? Edmund Wilson, otherwise a strong advocate of the book, alleged that the disaster is not significant enough in itself to serve as the catastrophe toward which the whole novel builds.[8] This scene is more adroit and more organic to the novel, however, than Wilson allows. Though Nona is the only one to suffer intensely, her suffering is genuine, and she is the most fully developed and sympathetic figure in the novel. She recoils from the concept of a loveless marriage that her mother advocates for her and the spurious loyalties implied in it. She also feels revulsion toward the hypocrisy of a society that hastens to deny realities such as treachery, adultery, and attempted murder in an effort to keep the surfaces of life pleasant and serene. Yet one might agree with Wilson's view that this climactic scene is not high tragedy. Nona is not murdered, nor is anyone else. Her future has not been inevitably destroyed. Consistent with the effects of tragicomedy, Nora can be expected to continue to love these people whom she cannot respect, and her retreat from society, we infer, will be only temporary.

Wharton did exactly right to end her novel with a ruthless exposé of the moral weakness of her central figures. If they were sensitive and self-conscious, the catastrophe would, of course, drastically affect them. But Wharton's point is precisely that insensitivity so completely encloses the modern rich that they cannot even recognize the scathing fires through which they walk. They are incapable of conceiving any conflict between morality and desire, they are impervious to the suffering of others, and they are unable to distinguish between the trivial and the notable. Even the cataclysm that they bring upon themselves is not recognized as a cataclysm; and something that more ordinary people would recognize as horrible they shrug off and cover up. "Twilight sleep"—the escape from pain and responsibility—is what they all want. They are inherently unsympathetic and, except for Nora, have been satirically dehumanized.

Among the characters, only Nona Manford rises above the spiritual limitations of her peers. She suffers in the brief climax of the novel with its threat of multiple murders because she refuses the anodyne of pleasure and irresponsibility that her world so freely offers. Rather, she experiences to the full a sense of outrage to her moral sensibilities as she acknowledges the others for what they are. Still, she is able to sympathize with them in their futile suffering even when they do not themselves realize that they are suffering; and, like a prophetess, she feels disaster closing in upon them all. When the catastrophe occurs, she alone cannot escape its consequences; her imaginative identification with all the friends and relatives involved in it paralyzes her spirit for a time; and she insists on going alone to the country to restore herself. Yet we must recognize that Nona's own sufferings and her satisfactions—her ability to appreciate nature, for instance—derive from an identical source—her full responsiveness to the life around her. Among the characters in the novel, only Nona, longing for the ideal, courageously confronts the real. She allows herself to love people, even though she knows they will fail her; and she achieves some of the self-knowledge that is indispensable for spiritual insight and for a true appraisal of her circumstances.

Nearly all the characters, except Nona, seek escape from boredom through excessive but aimless activity. Such escape activity is symbolized in Lita's orgiastic nude dances on the lawn of the estate of a "prophet" and in Pauline's recourse to an ultramodern fire engine, bought as a civic improvement project and complete with a nerve-blasting siren, to liven up her dinner party or to cover up an attempted murder. Whereas Nona responds to the beauty of a walk through the garden and the woods, her mother drives past her plantings quickly, admiring only her own efficiency: "Twenty-five thousand bulbs this year. . . . It was exhilarating to be always enlarging and improving . . . to face unexpected demands with promptness and energy."[9]

The aspect of modern life that Wharton most saliently satirizes in this novel is the attempt of the many to escape full knowledge and objective recognition of the world as it is. Hence there is irony in the cliché, which literary critics and historians circulated even before she died, that she herself sought in her life and the writings of her late years to escape from the realities of contemporary life. She may have wished to escape its deadening and distracting aspects, but she certainly knew, with an insider's knowledge, what it was she wished to avoid.

This novel presents best the increasingly uninhibited humor that Wharton allowed herself in her late novels. When Pauline, for example, addresses with exaggerated assurance the Birth Control League, she discovers that, because of a mistake in her appointment schedule, she is actually standing before the Mother's Day Committee. With imperturbable command and with almost admirable resourcefulness, she changes directions and adapts her planned remarks about contraception and the overworked mothers of large families to her "new" audience. Just as she reaches the edge of the abyss, she draws a quick breath and proceeds with, "That's what our antagonists say—the women who are afraid to be mothers, ashamed to be mothers, the women who put their . . . convenience . . . before the mysterious heaven-sent joy, the glorious privilege, of bringing children into the world" (*TS,* 113). She has avoided the dramatic closing remarks, planned for the Birth Control League, that refer to the vain sacrifices of mothers when illness claims the lives of the children they have borne. She donates money to an author because she finds one of his recent titles, *Beyond God,* "forward-looking," without realizing how patronizing and banal her own sentiments are.

In a description of the bungalows on the East River envisioned as a Viking-American settlement, Wharton lampooned the fad for cheap historical reproductions. To make her Viking home "authentic," Lita's aunt spends four years in research determining what kind of rushes the ancient explorers used for covering their floors; she will wait another fifty years to have the grasses woven in Abyssinia; and she refuses to own a clock lest she introduce an anachronism into her Viking abode.

If Wharton satirized the bogus quest for seeming authenticity, she also satirized the use of art as an escape from actuality. A bohemian friend of Lita's, to whom the real is "as tiresome as a truthful person," covers a window that provides a beautiful nightview of the Brooklyn Bridge with his picture of a brick wall and a fire escape. To such modernists, art must substitute for the real, not merely interpret it; and the substitute they offer springs from no creative depths in the artist. In *Twilight Sleep* and *The Children,* the comic devices, outrageous and farcical as they often are, intensify Wharton's acrid sense of the triviality of her characters. Mordant satire, not effervescent comedy, is, in reality, her mode of writing in these two novels.

Because of Wharton's control of multiple ironies in *Twilight Sleep,* Q. D. Leavis links the novel with Aldous Huxley's extravaganzas, such as *Antic Hay, Chrome Yellow, Point Counter Point,* and *Brave New World;* and she contends that *Twilight Sleep* compares favorably with them.[10] She also believes that all Wharton's satires, because they dramatize the lives of "rootless" people, provide an indispensable basis for understanding the fiction of such

young writers in the 1920s as F. Scott Fitzgerald, William Faulkner, and Kay
Boyle, who also explored the directionless lives of their contemporaries.
Leavis's judgment of Wharton's insight into the fruitless lives of the rich also
applies to her next novel, *The Children,* which appeared the year after *Twilight Sleep.*

The Children: Another Tragicomedy of Manners

The Children centers on the struggles of the seven Wheater children to
stay together after their much-divorced parents and stepparents have
shunted them from one household to another. The incongruities that develop between the innocence of the children and their poisoned experience
becomes Wharton's principal theme. Fifteen-year-old Judith Wheater,
who "mothers" the children, displays cynical sophistication about marriage,
adultery, alimony, and custody suits; but she remains a child in her illiterate
spelling, her love of games, and her pleasure in surprises and trivial gifts.
The adults swim, drink, and gamble on the Riviera. Whereas a lesser writer
might have surrounded them with glamour and excitement, Wharton recognizes that in their elaborate and anxious attempts to escape boredom, the
extremely rich are likely to be quarrelsome and dull. These adults, in an
ironic sense, may also be considered "the children" in the title of the novel.

But some adults in this world attempt to attain awareness and responsibility. Martin Boyne, for example, develops affection for the Wheater children
after a chance encounter with them on board ship. Before many weeks he
finds himself the guardian of the children, who are fighting to remain together without parental supervision; and he has lost enthusiasm for his approaching marriage to Rose Sellars, a beautiful and affluent widow. Though
he is a somewhat sensitive and perceptive man, his perceptiveness does not always include knowledge of his own emotions and motives. The women in the
novel, Judith Wheater and Rose Sellars, have more awareness concerning
human relationships than he has; and each likes to show that she is wiser
about the other than Boyne is. Hostility toward each other and a kind of fascination with each other as the scarcely admitted rivals for Boyne's attention
motivate the two women, one only fifteen and one middle-aged. Eventually
Boyne must be convinced—by Rose Sellars herself—that he has unconsciously fallen in love with Judith. When he proposes to her, Judith assumes
that he is teasing and laughs like a child at the idea of marriage. His ego is so
bruised by these encounters that he leaves both Mrs. Sellars and the children
to go to live in Brazil. In a melancholy epilogue, he returns three years later,

learns of the death of one of the children, watches Judith dancing with a young man, and silently leaves.

Although *The Children* recounts two love stories, each with some poignancy, the concept of love developed in it remains uncertain. The children gravely perceive all the adults as subject to "love storms," and they also assume that luck or fate will determine their own lives. For Martin Boyne and Rose Sellars, as well as for Judith Wheater and Martin, love does not reach fruition. The internal conflicts that preoccupy Martin and Rose are not vigorously defined or reconciled. Rose longs for an impulsive and overwhelming expression of her passion, but she clings desperately to "reason" as she feels herself drowning in the impracticality of Martin's daydreams. Martin sees himself staying indefinitely on the Riviera with the Wheater children, but he restlessly envisions himself attaining greatness by returning to his engineering projects, and he is horrified when Rose gently tries to make him see the depth of his attraction to the fifteen-year-old Judith. Although Wharton's attack on the irresponsibility of the wealthy Jazz Age parents is focused and determined, her handling of the two abortive love stories is tentative and exploratory. She poses questions but avoids conclusions to too great an extent. Martin and Rose renounce their engagement, and he leaves for Brazil, returning briefly after three years. He imagines Rose in New York, where she has returned to what he disdainfully calls her "past," and sees her graciously and always kindly serving her guests in an aristocratic society and presiding over social events. But he also sees her going about her routines with hands as transparent as those of a ghost and with eyes as empty, because she will live in the shadows where conventionally good and sheltered women dwell. A lonely man, he is aboard a boat to Brazil as the novel ends.

The ambivalence of the narrative, the indecisiveness of the main characters, and the ironic fates of the various children suggest that Wharton in this novel, as in *Twilight Sleep,* was more given to doubts about the meaning of life than she ever acknowledged. Nevertheless, one can infer that renunciation in love here has a positive value, providing both Martin and Rose with a degree of peace, security, and self-respect. Their renunciations link them to the characters in Wharton's fiction who give up the immediate happiness they long for because of personal and moral scruples—characters such as Anna Leath, George Darrow, and Sophy Viner in *The Reef,* Newland Archer and Ellen Olenska in *The Age of Innocence,* Nona Manford in *Twilight Sleep,* and Halo Tarrant in *The Gods Arrive* (although Halo apparently will reverse her decision). Such renunciations suggest Wharton's own withdrawal from the affair with Fullerton and reflect the insights into human nature that the ecstasy and the agony of that relationship had for her.

Wharton views her protagonist sympathetically, but he is not so self-assured as the bachelors of her fiction usually are. Though he is personable, he is something of an innocent, like the children for whom he develops such fondness. He selects flamboyant jewelry for Rose Sellars, a woman of conservative and sophisticated tastes: he has little sense of what is socially fitting. He is catapulted by his impulsiveness, his strong emotions, and his characteristic kindness into situations where his good intentions cause him to appear foolish. He becomes, at points, a ridiculous man whose frustrations seem as comic to the spectator as they must be frustrating to him. When he goes to the Lido to contend with the parents and stepparents (some eight or ten) who plan to separate the children, he cannot even get them all together long enough to talk; and the rapid sequence of scenes yields farcical effects. Once he corners nearly all of them in a hotel lobby; another time, in a tent on the beach. Finally—to his astonishment—they unanimously name him guardian just so that they can all run down the beach, like the larger children they themselves are, to watch a race.

Much of the humor related to Boyne arises from the contradiction between his image of himself as a heroic figure and the petty actualities that defeat him. He has an almost Byronic conception of his own emotional potential, but the responses of others to his pretensions always disappoint him. He feels that the fates conspire against him to prevent the right opportunity from arising for him to express his "greatness." Ironically, he fails to realize that it is not his image as a flamboyant personality but his good nature and genuine sympathy that are admirable and that awaken the genuine responses of others. Something of a romantic dreamer about himself, he would, he is certain, be able to savor fully the people and the situations about which he has fantasized were they to become actualities: "No tremor of thought or emotion would . . . have escaped Martin Boyne; he would have burst all the grapes against his palate."[11]

Instead, except for the lovely Rose Sellars whom Boyne never understands, he attracts only dull acquaintances, because he is dull without ever knowing it. In his travels he becomes closely associated with assorted types of people whom he really detests. Among the grotesques are an earnest lady in spectacles who is studying the background of Sicily before going there; an elderly man who each morning announces that he gets better bacon on board ship than he could possibly get at home; and a clergyman who—though his flock has paid for his vacation trip—plans not to visit the catacombs precisely because he is expected to do so (*TC,* 18). The humor inherent in Martin Boyne succeeds partly because Wharton liked him so much and was indulgent with him and partly because she caught a genuine comic type in him. The comedy in which he figures is sparked by his blunders, near-misses, mishaps, and discomfitures—all the result of good intentions that go wrong and leave him baffled.

The humorous effects that she attempted in the children are often brilliant but sometimes strained, especially those that result from their dialogue, which is at times inappropriate even for the stylized fiction with which she was experimenting. On the credit side, she generally kept the children from becoming adults in miniature, an achievement of which few authors can boast. On the whole, their conversation seems natural. But Wharton seems at times in handling the children to reach for the merely clever. For example, the children refer to their nurse, Miss Scope, as "horror-scope," and one child assumes her mother's best friend is "Sally Money" because she has so often heard her speak of alimony. Nevertheless, Wharton generally has a sharp ear for speech, especially when she re-creates the quarrels among the parents. She conveys consummately the boredom of Joyce Wheater, Judith's mother, when she has her murmur to her cigarette, "It's impossible to make Cliffe feel *nuances*" (53). She also has Joyce consider "her shining nails, as if glassing her indolent beauty in them" (*TC*, 151).

Wharton's failure to develop the relationship between Judith Wheater and the mature Rose Sellars is no doubt disappointing. If she had had more patience with her subject, she might have developed it with the power and insight she brought to *The Reef*, in which she fully explored the conflict between Sophy Viner and the mature Anna Leath. One wishes also that she had individualized Martin Boyne and Rose Sellars as fully as she had developed George Darrow and Anna Leath. Her failure in *The Children* to exhaust the psychic potential of this situation, indeed, prevents the novel from being more than a good one. We must grant that a novel of manners has stylized patterns that interfere with the full development of the characters, but Wharton could have penetrated more deeply and more subtly into the central situation than she does.

The externalized approach does provide some aesthetic compensations, however. The farcical nature of the principal scenes and the comic flavor with which Wharton invests her central characters, including Martin Boyne, provide a stark contrast not only to the poignant situations involving the children but also to the disappointments and painful bewilderment of the middle-aged lovers. Interspersed among the scenes of comic-fantasy are a few more somber and realistically envisioned situations involving somewhat more fully developed motivation and feelings in characters who still retain, as we have seen, some aura of the comic about them.

The rapid shifts from reality to artifice employed in *The Children* and *Twi-*

light Sleep led some readers to conclude that in these works Wharton had lost touch with the realities of modern life. These novels prove, rather, that she had kept abreast of the times and could judge some of the more blatant aspects of the postwar era for the shams they were. Her critics sometimes failed to see the caustic truth underlying her characters' heightened dialogue and her farcical distortions of character and situation. Both novels reveal that she retained intact a remarkable creative energy and a comic zest that allowed her to assimilate into satiric fiction a new and abrasive culture to which she was, in some respects, fundamentally antagonistic.

Chapter Eight
The Late Novels: 1929–1932

The Development of the Artist

In *Hudson River Bracketed* (1929) and *The Gods Arrive* (1932) Wharton recognized the changes wrought by the Great Depression on the everyday lives of Americans. Although critics tend to disregard these novels and although they are not among her greatest works, they hold a respectable place in the canon. Intellectually, they represent a culmination of many of her earlier preoccupations, for she dramatizes in these novels the artist's response to beauty, the struggle of the artist to find his own voice, his need to establish a meeting ground between the demands of integrity and the marketplace, the relationship of his vocation to his life as a person, the positive effects upon him of feminine interest in his work, and the destructive effects upon him of irresponsible passion. These two novels are in part the outcome of Wharton's extensive but often postponed plans for the never-completed novel *Literature,* which was begun in 1913 and which was to have traced the development of a writer. Conversations in these two novels also provide a significant reflection of her views on trends in literature during her later years and are therefore essential to a full understanding of her aesthetic views and practice.

The novels chronicle Vance Weston's emergence as a writer from his first short story to his successful novels, but they also chronicle the closely related subject of his love life. His first relationship ends in disillusionment with the promiscuous Floss Delaney in Euphoria, Illinois; and this affair is succeeded by a disturbing marriage to lovely but dependent Laura Lou Tracy, who dies at the end of the first book. Thereafter, and at the heart of both novels, is his life with Halo Tarrant, who inspires him as a platonic influence in the first book and who becomes his mistress in the second. Throughout the two novels, Wharton focuses intensively both on Vance Weston's achievement of identity as a writer and on his growing awareness as a man.

After Vance's abortive relationship with Floss, he leaves the Midwest to live with his distant relatives, the Tracys, in rural New York. He is relatively innocent and hopes to become a writer by absorbing the sophisticated influences of New York City. To his dismay, he is disappointed in all such expectations when he finds himself in a run-down house in a rural area at some distance from the city, an area which, if anything, is more isolated and backward than his home town. His impoverished relatives clean and care for The Willows, which was described in an 1842 book on architecture as the best example of Hudson River Bracketed, an ornate style characterized by irregular narrow balconies supported by wooden brackets. The Willows is crucial to Vance's career, though he does not at first realize this. In the tiny library at The Willows, he discovers the "Past" and becomes convinced that, through familiarity with the literary tradition he can gain by perusing the old books there, he will become, like Samuel Taylor Coleridge, a distinguished writer. Halo Spear, a relative of the Tracys, who is a few years older than Vance, eagerly volunteers to be his intellectual guide as he plans to immerse himself in the classics.

Intellectual ambition does not represent for Vance the only fulfillment. His emotional nature also demands recognition; and as a result, he persuades the gentle, naive Laura Lou Tracy to break her engagement to the enterprising Bunny Hayes and to elope with him. Their relationship, far from harmonious, is tragic for Laura Lou. Because Vance has to discipline himself in order to write, he ignores her loneliness. A complication supervenes when Vance retreats to The Willows in search of a more relaxing atmosphere for writing each day. Halo begins to meet him regularly to help him with his novel.

Local gossips, particularly Mrs. Tracy, interpret these meetings to Laura Lou as sexual infidelity. Dissension between husband and wife reaches a new intensity when Vance takes Laura Lou to the city after his first success. While he makes the rounds of social and literary New York and becomes involved in maneuvering for an important prize, Laura Lou lives a lonely existence in a boardinghouse. Halo Spear's husband, Lewis Tarrant, a magazine editor, hires Vance, exploits him financially, and eventually fires him. Though Vance's first novel sells phenomenally, he receives little money from it.

Toward the end of *Hudson River Bracketed,* Vance and Laura Lou find an abandoned house at the edge of the city and live there in extreme poverty for months. So as not to disturb Vance's frustrating work on another novel, Laura Lou heroically hides the fact that she is hemorrhaging from tuberculosis. In the closing scene of *Hudson River Bracketed,* Halo Spear finds the Westons after much searching, announces to Vance that she has separated from Tarrant, and learns a moment later that Laura Lou has just died. Halo's arrival anticipates the second book, in which Wharton details Halo's life with Vance, particularly as it relates to their troubled personal relationship and her attempts to shape his work.

Blake Nevius declares that not one of the many artists in Wharton's work bears the stamp of authenticity.[1] This overstates the case, although it is true that both these novels are more concerned with the women Vance loves, with his social position, and with his constant struggle for economic survival than they are with his mastery of his craft. He does, however, provide a voice through which Wharton can express her views, and his activities and struggles as a writer are grim enough. In fact, Wharton's involvement with Vance makes him, in some respects, the most believable and interesting artist in her fiction. Granted that she satirizes Vance's adolescent romanticism as he finds himself inspired by "that celestial Beauty which haunted earth and sky and the deeps of his soul" and that she tends at such times to forget his mundane responsibilities, he emerges as her most authentic spokesman because he is not idealized.

Through Vance, Wharton reiterates some principles about literature that she held throughout her career, such as the artist's obligation to select detail and his need to reveal a structural sense in his work. In the two books she also voices through him or through his mentor, Halo Spear, her views on the literature of the 1920s and 1930s. When either Vance or Halo expresses sensible views on the nature of literature, a loquacious writer or editor advances opposing ideas. The result is a further exposition of some of Vance's or Halo's principles in the form of a literary dialogue with spirited antagonists. Vance and Halo denounce the superficiality of young writers who are commercially ambitious, the pessimism of naturalist authors, and the fragmentation of personality that Wharton felt was induced in a character by the use of the stream of consciousness technique. Vance certainly speaks for her whenever he discusses writing, especially when he tries to analyze his problems as a writer of fiction. In her description through Vance of the creative process, Wharton echoes Henry James's idea of the donnée from which all else is derived. The imagination builds on a single fragment of fact—a single kernel that the author then separates from all others and plants in his mind to grow independently.

The artist must learn to observe economy both in his personal life and in his art, for they depend on each other. Vance learns this principle of moderation in all things as he leaves The Willows after his first visit. Wharton relates this principle to the action at several points in *The Gods Arrive* because Halo's failure to understand it precipitates the rift between her and Vance and causes some of Vance's problems and misfortunes. Too much intense experience upsets Vance; his abnormally keen sensibility can only accommodate a certain amount of stimulation if he is to do his best work: "When the impressions were too abundant and powerful, they benumbed him."[2] In Spain, for instance,

Vance grows lazy and seems to lose even his desire to store his sensations for future use precisely because they are too abundant here for him to value correctly. We suspect that Wharton suffered from a similar surfeit of experience during World War I, when she postponed indefinitely the actual composition of "Literature" and of other novels.

When Vance visits Chartres, he suspects that he may already have heard too much about its sublimity. Not surprised that his reactions to it are dulled, he is bitterly disappointed that he has lost his capacity to respond to a monument he recognizes with his intellect to be a great work of art. He is later reassured when he is able to react spontaneously to the simpler beauty of a small church in which he seeks refuge during a storm. In the lightning flashes he glimpses a "fragment of heaven" and sits "among these bursts of glory and passages of darkness as if alternate cantos of the *Paradiso* and the *Inferno* were whirling through him" (*GA,* 80–81). Just as the childhood memory of the River Dudden inspired the adult William Wordsworth, so the mere sights and sounds of a river can become for Vance the small, secreted treasures that feed creativity.

Wharton frequently refers, through Vance's voice, to the problems a young writer encounters in trying to maintain his originality and independence. Critics, editors, the influence of other writers, and even the reading of books are all suspect. Vance distrusts critics because, as Halo remarks, they change their standards every day. Halo and, somewhat later, Vance suspect the disinterestedness of editors because they apply, by and large, commercial criteria to their judgment of art. Editors discourage Vance from being original, preferring him to write in the future what has sold well in the past: "the principle of the quick turnover applied to brains as it was to real estate." In her own essays, Wharton found it troubling that some of her younger contemporaries refused to read great literature lest they endanger their originality and become derivative in their art. Halo, like Wharton, sees immersion in the tradition as essential to a writer; and she magisterially comments about the New York literary set that "the clever young writers . . . had read only each other and *Ulysses*" (*GA,* 46).

As a young writer, Vance faces frustration because he can easily copy the facile improvisations and stylistic tricks of his contemporaries but longs to communicate his own vision of the world and his sense of the stark forces that determine man's fate. Wharton herself as a younger writer was undoubtedly annoyed by reviewers who spoke of her cleverness and epigrammatic prose when she was trying to probe deeply into human problems. Vance voices the young author's self-doubt as to whether a book composed easily can be good and whether a best-seller can have lasting value.

Wharton's own work shows little correlation between the time and effort spent on a novel and its financial success. She herself refused to value as her best works those that sold best. But even in the 1920s she felt the same frustration that Vance voices as to the difficulty of evaluating one's own work in the light of hostile criticism.

Again like Wharton in her critical works, Vance distrusts the stream of consciousness technique, popular among the other young writers in Paris and New York. In *The Gods Arrive,* his friends contend that "the art of narrative and the portrayal of social groups had reached its climax" and that now the only hope for attaining new dimensions in fiction lay in "the exploration of the subliminal" (*GA,* 112). But Wharton, to the end, saw the use of a structured plot and of dialogue as more effective methods of characterization than the random probing of the inner psyche; and she rebelled against the formlessness, as she saw it, of stream of consciousness fiction.

For Vance—and probably also for Wharton—the stream of consciousness technique was inevitably associated with a deterministic pessimism, derived in large part from the literary naturalists, though originally these naturalists had not made much use of the detailed examination of the inner psyche or experimented much with form. Although Wharton's own work as early as *The House of Mirth* showed the influence of naturalism, she never fully subscribed to its deterministic tenets because, in Vance's words, stream of consciousness fiction tends to reduce characters "to a bundle of loosely tied instincts and habits, borne along blindly on the current of existence" (*GA,* 112), and inevitably, therefore, to minimize their powers of free choice. Like his most sensitive contemporaries, Vance wants to depict reality as it is, no matter how somber; but he wants to see a whole man "pitted against a hostile universe, and surviving, and binding it to his own uses" (*GA,* 113).

Wharton also felt that naturalist novelists tended to create characters so sensational or grotesque that they soon degenerated into stereotypes. She expressed her dissatisfaction with this tendency in many of her contemporaries through a young Englishman, Chris Churley, and his comments about current American writing. He derides the two extremes in popular fiction, romantic historical novels and documentary naturalist novels, because both offer up undeveloped characters. He does not understand, furthermore, why modern writers disregard in their work the middle class, which comprises so much that is essentially American; instead, these authors choose to write about princesses in Tuscan villas or ignorant peasants, "gaunt young men with a ten-word vocabulary who spend their lives sweating and hauling

wood. . . . There's really nothing as limited as the primitive passions—
except perhaps those of the princesses" (*GA,* 176).

The Satire of the Superficial and the Provincial

Beyond her views on literature, Wharton expressed through Vance her
scorn for time-serving authors and the venality that motivates them. Her satire may be excessive in depicting the young writers and artists at the Loafers
Club and the Coconut Tree Restaurant in New York or at Lorry Spear's
apartment in Paris. They are at least dedicated to what they are doing despite
their superficiality and false sophistication. But her ridicule of current modes
of writing fiction is inescapable and amusing, if a bit too broad and farcical.
The tendencies she condemned perhaps did not deserve all the attention she
awarded them. But, when her young writers discuss the popular novel *Price
of Meat,* now in its seventieth thousand, or *Egg Omelette* (the latter's sales
boosted by pulpit denunciations of it), they demonstrate how ridiculous any
fad in art can become. Likewise, the quarrel of a prize committee over a
book's "exact degree of indecency" and the maneuvering by writers and publishers for the Pulsifer Prize are amusing and contemporaneous aspects of
Hudson River Bracketed and *The Gods Arrive.* They recall the machinations
of George Gissing's characters in the literary world of the 1890s in *New Grub
Street,* as well as the failure of Sinclair Lewis to win the Pulitzer Prize for *Main
Street.*

The high-powered parties designed to promote the sales of books and
to publicize the reputations of writers also come under Wharton's steady
scrutiny—parties, for example, in which a woman presses an author to identify the originals of his characters and to verify her suspicion that his love
scenes reflect his personal life. With the good humor born of long experience
with book promotions, she can even laugh indulgently in *Hudson River
Bracketed* at the publicity given to books by newspaper interviews with authors: "The heart-to-heart kind. . . . With a snapshot of yourself looking at
the first crocus in your garden; or smoking a pipe, with your arm round a
Great Dane."[3]

If Wharton's satire here is often biting and precise, at other times it is mal-
adroit, even crude, less controlled than that in *Twilight Sleep* and *The Children.* In her depiction of the rich, ostentatious tourists in *The Gods Arrive,* she
attacks them too directly and harshly; she seems oblivious to the possibility
that her attack might be outdated because the United States was in the
depths of the depression when this novel appeared and most of the wealthy
people of the 1920s had become impoverished. Her satire seems out of place

in such comments as "If you're going to buy a Rolls-Royce, buy two—it pays in the end" or "We've run down a little place *at last* where you can really count on the caviar" (*GA,* 215).

Even more difficult to defend is her snobbish treatment of Vance's midwestern background and his lack of literary sophistication. For a college graduate interested in the arts, he is impossibly ignorant of literature; American colleges could not have been so provincial as Wharton makes them out to be. So his remark to Halo, a stranger, when he skims a book by Coleridge, "Why wasn't I ever told about the Past before?" is totally false (*HRB,* 50). American education in those days would have done better by Vance than to acquaint him only with James Whitcomb Riley, Ella Wheeler Wilcox, John Greenleaf Whittier, Henry Wadsworth Longfellow, James Russell Lowell, and a little Walt Whitman. As a cultured Easterner, Halo Spear is ignorantly disdainful of the Midwest and its purported lack of culture; she imagines that Vance's classmates in the sixth grade were young "savages" about to "maul" "The Ancient Mariner" and other selections in their readers. Though Wharton amuses readers with her choice of names—such as Prune, Nebraska, and Hallelujah, Missouri—her ridicule of the Midwest through her derision of the forces and the milieu that have molded her central character misfires. If Vance is an original genius, as Wharton would argue, his region must have contributed more to his development than she is willing to admit.

Yet Wharton does show some sympathy for small-town life and regards some aspects of it with indulgent humor. Vance's father, the real estate promoter (who names his son "Advance" after his land development in Missouri), and Vance's mother and sisters, with their concern for status, are authentic representatives of the small town. Their bungalow living room reflects Wharton's interest in interiors and is typical of middle-class homes in any town in the United States at this time. The gold and gray wallpaper, the phonograph on the library table, the crocheted tablecloth, the religious pictures in Woolworth frames, and the houseplant on a milking stool were ubiquitous "props" in 1930. Realistic, too, and humorous is the general evasiveness characterizing the funeral when quotations from Isaiah and James Whitcomb Riley are "intermingled with a practiced hand" and the word "died" is replaced by "passed over."

The success of Wharton's presentation of provincial life is to be measured largely in terms of the skill with which she envisions her minor characters, Grandpa and Grandma Scrimser, for example. Grandma's ranging and mercurial evangelism is suddenly in demand for lectures in the living rooms of wealthy women in New York. She is an older and more solid version of Pauline Manford in *Twilight Sleep* and of Julia Brant in *A Son at the Front.*

An elderly "new woman," Grandma scandalizes her children and grandchildren by her uninhibited behavior. This time the children of a wayward parent are scandalized, not the parents of wayward children. As an evangelist, Grandma is an interesting variation on the religious charlatan in Wharton's other fiction and in Sinclair Lewis's *Elmer Gantry.* She is more sincere than the evangelists who are typically satirized and believes that she gives something of value to the people whose money she takes. She does, however, confide to Vance that baking gingerbread to sell to her neighbors in Missouri was harder work than "coaxing folks back to Jesus."

Grandpa Scrimser, more unscrupulous, is a variation on the elderly small-town lecher. As a youth, Vance experiences much revulsion when he discovers that Floss Delaney is Scrimser's mistress as well as his own. But Vance comes to pity as well as hate Grandpa when a stroke fells the old man and Vance takes him home from the hotel bar; he is a pitiable figure, "like a marionette with its wires cut, propped on the sofa to which they had hurriedly raised him" (*HRB,* 146). Ironically, when Vance returns to Euphoria as a successful author, he visits with Floss Delaney in the remodeled bar of the hotel (which she now owns) and realizes that Floss seems to have forgotten Grandpa's very existence.

Although in these two books Wharton lacks the perceptiveness and practical detachment that characterize her satire in earlier works, she reveals, nevertheless, a remarkable capacity to document a social group, to create minor characters in a quick phrase or two, and to evoke a milieu entirely appropriate to the individuals and the events that dominate the novels.

Halo Spear: The Dilemma of the "New Woman"

In *The Gods Arrive,* Wharton concentrates on the relationship between Halo Tarrant and Vance Weston that had begun early in *Hudson River Bracketed* before Vance's marriage to Laura Lou. The relationship, as Wharton portrays it, lacks some dimension of veracity, though it is full of interest in many ways. There are some inconsistencies and weaknesses in Vance's characterization. Wharton does less well with Halo Spear and seems unable to attain a viable balance between the opposing forces in her character; as a result, Halo emerges as a less sympathetic individual than Wharton intended her to be. Wharton is perhaps not critical enough of Halo's unscrupulousness, her materialism, and her selfishness. Halo hardly represents the graciousness of tradition when she argues that her family would have difficulty conversing at dinner if they were to invite their poor relatives, the Tracys, along with Vance: "They talk another language and it can't be helped" (*HRB*, 87). Condescension and a certain envy mark her attitude toward Vance's creative work from the moment she interrupts his reading at The Willows on his first visit, yet Wharton inconsistently regards her as one whose real gift is "for appreciating the gifts of others" (*HRB*, 84). Other aspects of her actions and motivations also seem to be contradictions that Wharton does not reconcile, rather than complexities that add richness to Halo's character.

Fortunately, Halo Spear in *The Gods Arrive* is not the same woman she was in *Hudson River Bracketed*, and this change may be partly, if not entirely, explained by her having attained greater experience and maturity. In the earlier book, she had shown a servile willingness to marry Lewis Tarrant for his money and prestige and for the opportunity marriage gives her to leave Paul's Landing for New York City, and Wharton tends to equate Halo's limited economic opportunities with those available to Lily Bart at the turn of the century in *The House of Mirth*: "Even had discipline and industry fostered her slender talents they would hardly have brought her a living . . . what else was there for her but marriage?" (*HRB*, 84). This total lack of confidence in Halo's ability to earn her own living is inconsistent with the impression that Halo elsewhere conveys of being a character who has enough confidence in herself to bolster Vance's faltering ego in his struggles to realize himself as a writer.

In *The Gods Arrive*, Halo is nothing if not independent; a "new woman," she prefers not to marry Vance, even after Tarrant reluctantly grants her a divorce. Together she and Vance tour Europe for the sake of providing him with inspiration and subject matter for his books. Though society insults and excludes her, Halo refuses to impose sexual and social restrictions on her lover, and Wharton's own ambivalent feelings about the value of marriage probably appear here. When Halo declares that she wants Vance to feel as free as air, she is reminded paradoxically that a woman who refuses to marry may be chaining her lover all the tighter: "The defenseless woman, and all that. If you were his wife, you and he'd be on a level" (*GA*, 313). The situation in which a woman idealizes her role as mistress when a man advocates marriage had appeared early and frequently in Wharton's short stories and had reappeared in the 1920s in both *A Son at the Front* and *Twilight Sleep*. In *The Gods Arrive*, Wharton might have been commenting subtly on the fact that American men were thought to be more chivalrous to the unmarried women they loved than to their wives.

Halo's experiences as Vance's mistress are both inspiriting and distressing. She defends herself vigorously against the criticism of her brother Lorry, who hypocritically resents her visiting him, although he lives with a mistress as do his bohemian friends in Paris: "Naturally a man feels differently about his sister." With some conviction, Wharton presents marriage not as a more virtuous alternative to free love but as a stabilizing institution that prevents a person's life from becoming unduly chaotic. Marriage keeps life in balance, as Frenside, the wise philosopher, declares: "We most of us need a framework, a support—the maddest lovers do. Marriage may be too tight a fit—may dislocate and deform. But it shapes life too; prevents lopsidedness or drifting" (*GA*, 311). Marriage also becomes a kind of insurance against the inevitable breaking up of strong love—the cynical, but humane, answer to the sometimes ephemeral nature of sexual love. Marriage, by retaining the mere forms of love, prevents the violent tearing up of dying roots, which may still on occasion be reinvigorated. Vance finally sees marriage as providing a way for two people who have once filled each other's universe to hold together as the tide of natural passion and intense involvement recedes.

Actually, it is Halo's intellectual superiority—sometimes presented as genuine, at other times as specious—that jeopardizes their relationship. The love affair runs aground when Vance comes to resent Halo's dominating influence on his writing and intellectual growth. The appearance of his old flame, Floss Delaney, for whom surprisingly he feels some of his former passion revive, threatens further complications.

Halo's relationship to Vance provides the major focus of the novel, and it is a relationship characterized by much poignancy despite Halo's occasional limitations as a person. For her, sex indissolubly merges with her interest in Vance as an artist; and she can hardly think of love in any terms other than intellectual. She buries her own ambition in order to support her lover's, only to find that he becomes increasingly restive under the pressure she exerts. To Halo, the man must succeed in order to satisfy the woman who stands behind him and who finds her aspirations satisfied vicariously by his success. The compulsion on the man in such a case may become unbearable, however, as it does with Vance.

Vance's frustrated love and his desertion of Halo arise from his resentment of the intellectual and artistic pressures she thrusts upon him, although her interest in his writing had fostered their early love and contributed signally to his success. He had responded sexually to her in *Hudson River Bracketed* when he first sensed that her imagination was flowing through his and inflaming him as he planned his first novel. In *The Gods Arrive*, she has had to become more passive in her influence: "she listened intelligently, but she no longer collaborated" (*GA*, 72). To this extent, her love as she envisioned it has diminished; she is apparently no longer the chief source of her lover's inspiration; and he may, in fact, have developed beyond her powers to bring him out further. She can never fully accept his view, expressed several months later, of the artist's need for independence from the criticism of others: "My dear child—shall I give you the cold truth . . . the artist asks other people's opinions to please *them* and not to help himself" (*GA*, 337).

Because Halo insists on loving the artist as well as the man, her love becomes finally, and ironically, a repressive influence upon the man she is straining to serve. For him, she becomes "a reproach and a torment," when all he wants is to collect his own thoughts in contemplative peace: "The absorbing interest of seeing his gift unfold under her care had been so interwoven with her love that she could not separate them" (*GA*, 28). A kind of masochism underlies her wish to be subservient to his talent as she asks herself, " 'Shall I have to content myself with being a peg to hang a book on?' and found an anxious joy in the idea" (*GA*, 36). Vance resents her expectant watching for his reactions to new experience, her monitoring of his progress as a potential artist. At Chartres, he grows sulky and baffled and declares he cannot see what she expects him to see. It is as if he has failed her sexual demands and become suddenly impotent before a curious and excessively sympathetic woman: "Halo was elaborately tactful; she waited, she kept silent; she left him to his emotions; but no emotions came. . . . The masculine longing to be left alone was uppermost; he wanted to hate Chartres without having to give any reason" (*GA*, 78–79).

Halo's smothering care of Vance extends even to his manuscripts. The result is that his frustrations—and her suffering from his rejection—intensify. His books for her become phallic emblems when she judges each new work in terms of its relationship to his masculinity. She resents any lesser book of his as a kind of sexual affront to her, as though it were a symbol of personal weakness and depleted vigor on Vance's part and an insult to her own protective femininity: "What business had a man of Weston's quality to be doing novels like ladies' fancy-work. . . . The next book . . . will show them all what he really is. . . . There were times when she caught herself praying for that next book as lonely wives pray for a child" (*GA*, 85–86). Later, when she fears that he may merely be following literary fashion in his new novel, instead of expressing his individuality as she knows it, she resents his hiding the manuscript from her; and she equates such furtiveness with a husband's hiding the evidence of sexual infidelity. She refuses to look at the manuscript, just as she would refuse to spy on an affair: "If there had been a letter from a woman in that drawer, she reflected, it would have been almost easier to resist looking at it" (*GA*, 100).

Wharton handles with sympathy and insight Vance's desertion of Halo and her sufferings from this separation in the last chapters of *The Gods Ar-*

rive. Halo simply returns to The Willows, where her supreme adventure with Vance had begun, and mechanically devotes herself to gardening. She refuses to think or feel, and she only responds to the heat of the sun on her neck and the fatigue in her muscles. She tries to kill her suffering by not allowing it to surface to her conscious mind and by resolutely turning her energies to physical pursuits.

Halo's final recognition that Vance has resented her part in his work is more bitter to her than the waning of his passion. Cynically, she had acknowledged that passion cannot last, but she had had faith that a deeper understanding underlay their particular love. "The intellectual divorce" between them became more bitter to her than their physical separation. Conversely, the fact that Halo has allowed this intellectual divorce to occur frees Vance for a renewal of his passion for Halo in the last scene, in which he discovers she is pregnant and approaches her simply as a child approaches a protective maternal figure. He wishes her to protect him and to be, in a sense, a mother to him as well as to the child that they have conceived. Vance is not yet ready to accept the intellectual companionship of a woman, though, as a sensitive man, he may eventually be able to do so. In the last scene, he sees her as at one with the soil and the sun in her garden. She is back in "the Past" at The Willows, and she is at one with nature in her pregnancy. She has, in these respects, fulfilled the romantic dreams that Vance previously associated with her. Perhaps the sincerity that imbues his romanticism will also develop in the future into a full appreciation of Halo's distinction, for Halo has been refined and matured by the suffering she has in part brought on herself.

The Buccaneers: An Old Theme, a New Hope

In *The Buccaneers* (1938) Wharton returned to the theme she had developed in many shorter works and in her greatest novels: *The House of Mirth, The Custom of the Country,* and *The Age of Innocence*—the comparative value of modernity and tradition. Like *The Age of Innocence, The Buccaneers* takes place in the 1870s; but more in this than in any of her earlier novels Wharton emphasizes the positive qualities in young Americans, the conscientiousness and seriousness in the children of the rising middle class, and takes a more satiric approach to European nobility. Reflecting the milieu of the 1930s as well as that of the 1870s, she reveals her own concern for the welfare of workers and their families in her treatment of a disagreement between the young Duke and Duchess of Tintagel.

The buccaneers are five young American women—Lizzie and Mab Elmsworth, Virginia and Annabel (Nan) St. George, and Conchita Closson.

They enliven a Saratoga summer resort, while their ambitious mothers sit on the porches of the lodge, fanning themselves, eyeing other guests critically, and wondering what the menu in the hotel dining room will be. No less ambitious socially, but wanting more excitement, their fathers closely watch for glamorous women guests and new business prospects.

The individualism and the eagerness for change that characterize the buccaneers promise an invigorating and freshening force in European as well as American society. Disappointed the next winter in their attempts to crash New York society, the energetic buccaneers decide to conquer London and marry into the nobility. Their high spirits, their defiance of stodgy conventions, and their determination to win what they want lend their enterprise a vitality and a confidence that contrast with the complacency of the conservative older generation in both America and England. Miss Laura Testvalley, the thirty-nine-year-old Italian governess of Nan St. George, directs the campaign; and she also provides the indispensable link between the two generations. Although the tone of the novel is usually light and ingratiating, Wharton's insistent irony modulates the comedy because the men and the society that the buccaneers conquer are, after all, not really worthy of their beauty, intelligence, and courageous spirits.

Wharton spent her last four or five years writing the fragment; it was published the year after her death with her plot outline and a long essay, "A Note on *The Buccaneers*," by Gaillard Lapsley.[4] By the end of the fragment, one of the women has married a civil servant, and the others have married British noblemen. Most important, Nan St. George has been for some time the Duchess of Tintagel; has suffered a miscarriage; has just fallen in love with a baronet, Guy Thwarte; and has announced her intention to divorce the Duke of Tintagel. The synopsis indicates that Wharton intended that Nan would leave her husband, the duke, and elope with the baronet, Guy Thwarte, and that Laura Testvalley would sacrifice her own chances for a good marriage with Sir Helmsley Thwarte by assisting in this elopement of his son and a divorced woman. The fragment deviates from the author's synopsis in that the Elmsworth girls figure less prominently in the novel than they do in the plan; Miss Testvalley, who had seemed destined to be the protagonist in the synopsis, becomes relatively minor in her function in the plot, although she is a fascinating personality; and Nan St. George becomes the chief character.

Gaillard Lapsley expressed misgivings about publishing the unfinished work of an author so given to extensive revision, but he decided that the several existing sections should not be withheld and that publication would give readers an insight into the work of a careful craftsman at a midpoint in the creation of an important work. Louis Auchincloss dismisses *The Buccaneers* as a novel just as well left unfinished.[5] On the other hand, Geoffrey Walton has viewed the book as the work that would have been most significant in the last twenty years of Wharton's career had she completed it.[6] He thinks it would have equalled her early masterpieces, and he sees in it a new revelation of her need to achieve a social reintegration by balancing the traditions and dignity of the Old World with the sincerity and energy of the New. To him, Wharton's vision of an emerging harmony between the classes would have possessed intellectual weight and emotional richness.

Much of what can be said about an uncompleted work must be based on an assumption of what the finished work would have become, but the possibility remains that Wharton might have made this novel her most interesting one since *The Age of Innocence*. Certainly Nan Tintagel and Laura Testvalley would have been strong characters; and Ushant, the Duke of Tintagel, even in the present sketch of him, is one of her finest minor characters. Wharton in the early part of the book takes a slightly amused view of her characters and their social ambitions. A good-natured tone underlies her descriptions, for instance, of Mrs. St. George sipping her lemonade on the veranda of the Saratoga hotel while she looks forward to entering the dining room with her husband because he is the most handsome man in the hotel. But her excessive pride in him makes her vulnerable to fears that all the women in the resort are conspiring to win him from her, especially some whom she vaguely identifies as "the dreadful painted women . . . who leered and beckoned . . . under the fringes of their sunshades" and other more fashionable ladies whom she characterizes as ones who wear pink bonnets. Mrs. St. George herself would like to be more stylish, but she longs for the good old days when fashion flattered the slightly plump—with crinoline petticoats and dresses "looped up at the hem like drawing-room draperies." The broomlike silhouette now in style, with all the material gathered at the hips, she sees as another conspiracy against her. If Wharton treats Mrs. St. George with some ridicule, she is compassionate in understanding her fears and her isolation when she must leave her husband to accompany the buccaneers on their European campaign.

The Europeans, as well as the Americans, are the subject of the same friendly satire, though it at times carries more sting. The Duke of Tintagel, who loves to repair clocks, absentmindedly forgets his mission, no matter where he is, if he finds a clock not working properly. He holds it to his ear as gently and as thoughtfully as a doctor does his stethoscope when he is diagnosing a heart condition. Having greatness thrust upon him by inheritance, he longs to be an ordinary citizen who can simply wind his own clocks in peace. Wharton also depicts the duke's father with kindly ridicule: "The late Duke had had no vices; but his virtues were excessively costly" (*TB*, 165).

Among other costs imposed by his accepting too seriously the responsibilities of his dukedom, the old duke had fathered eight daughters in the tedious attempt to produce an heir.

Lord Brightlingsea, who becomes father-in-law to two of the buccaneers, can never remember without his wife's prompting who Miss March is. Yet Miss March is the American whom he jilted at the church door some twenty-five years before and who has devotedly remained in England for the pleasure of watching his family grow up.

The latter half of the fragment successfully exploits the mockheroic approach. Conchita Closson, already married to Lord Seadown, leaves for England and establishes a military outpost for the campaign soon to be launched by the others. Laura Testvalley, upon landing in England, becomes a scout to survey the territory before battle plans are drawn. She calls upon Miss March and enlists the defeated soldier of the last generation in another battle of American women against English noblemen. Miss March sits in her little London house planning her strategy; she is eager to play a secret part in a new adventure, for she feels a kinship with these young "marauders."

The high point of the warfare occurs when Lady Churt descends upon the young women in the garden at Runnymede in a fit of jealousy, and a fiery scene ensues. Lady Churt, who has rented her cottage to the buccaneers, discovers that her lover, Lord Richard, is still a frequent guest at the cottage in her absence because he is attracted to both Lizzie Elmsworth and Virginia St. George. When the invader in her fury seems to be besting the buccaneers and the embarrassed Lord Richard, Lizzie, who has been jealous of Virginia, suddenly joins forces with her against the enemy; and she suggests in an imperious tone that it is the proper moment for Lord Richard and Virginia to announce their engagement. Routed by this strategy, Lady Churt and her straggling troops find their way back to her motorcar.

The novel remains hilarious and farcical in its fast movement. We recognize that the buccaneers gain the field against an enemy more than willing to be conquered—the enemy who are men. However, a more serious tone pervades the scenes near the end in which Nan Tintagel plans to divorce her husband of almost two years because she is in love with Sir Guy Thwarte. With the book as it presently exists, we can find no adequate justification for the divorce. Ushant, the Duke of Tintagel, can be accused only of dullness and ultraconservatism, and Wharton has made him a likable, if inept, character. Certainly in endorsing Nan's elopement, Wharton was going beyond the mores of 1870 and also beyond her own views about the situations that justify divorce or desertion. When divorce occurs in the life of a sympathetic character in her fiction, a strong reason exists for it, and her fictional interest in such cases most often centers on the problems resulting from the divorce or the desertion rather than on the situation that generated the marital discord. In this case, the probable marriage of Nan and Guy Thwarte seems symbolic of a kind of union of two societies, American and English, and as a strong new fusion of the forces of tradition and change. Both parties to the new marriage have pursued at the same time the materialistic and the aesthetic without experiencing any sense of futility or conflict.

As to the British aristocracy, Wharton is not without sympathy for it, in spite of her awareness of its occasional moral weaknesses and opportunism. She shows respect for the English nobility in its interest in family stability, in its efficient management of households, in its maintenance of beautiful and historic homes, and in its sense of responsibility to the surrounding community. Nevertheless, she is also aware of the absurdities involved when an impoverished nobleman resorts to all kinds of hypocritical expedients to maintain the family estate and when the same nobleman rationalizes his ignoring the general needs of a community by bestowing token benefits on the laborers on his estates. Although Geoffrey Walton sees "fantastic ignorance, frequent absurdity, and breath-taking hypocrisy" in the British aristocrats in this novel,[7] we also find these same (or similar) characteristics in the newly rich parents of the buccaneers who are invading the British strongholds. The hope set forth in the book would seem to lie less in the influence of Americans on the English than in the emergence of a new kind of young people in both nations who value tradition and art at the same time that they seek change in social patterns.

The direction of the book indicates the error of those who suggest that Wharton's skill in the writing of fiction had left her before her death and that, in the latter part of her life, she longed only for the settled past, viewed the present with dissatisfaction, and thought of the future with foreboding. In her seventies, she was a writer whose technical expertise was still developing and whose fictional resources had by no means been depleted.

Chapter Nine

Wharton's Art: Alive beyond Her "Mortal Lease"

Wharton's two books published soon after her death, *The Buccaneers* (1938) and *Ghosts* (1937), broaden our understanding of her later life and works. Although Wharton did not live to finish *The Buccaneers,* her editor, Gaillard Lapsley, apparently understood her intentions and edited it carefully for publication. Wharton wrote one of her best stories, "All Souls," expressly for her final short story collection, *Ghosts;* she provided for the volume the only preface she ever wrote for a collection of her stories; and she apparently surprised everyone by dedicating it with high praise to Walter de la Mare. The quality of these two posthumously published books almost immediately projected her published works beyond her lifetime, and they indicate how completely she was dedicated to artistic achievement to the close of her life. Certainly *The Buccaneers* is suffused with a new hope as she presents against a historical background what was for her an old theme.

Aspiring always to understand complex human problems, Wharton in her fiction dramatized most frequently those issues related to the status of women and to the limiting effects of convention on individual development. In her fiction she also confronted hidden psychological fears, including those related to supernatural mysteries, and she pondered the possibility or impossibility of men and women ever finding love that blends the elements of sex, companionship, and intellectual compatibility. She does not provide solutions to these complex problems but sheds much light on them all. Her persistence in addressing them, in questioning old assumptions, in comparing alternative choices to human dilemmas, and in exposing individual weaknesses and evasiveness illuminates manifold aspects of the human situation. From her autobiography, letters, and the observations of her contemporaries, we see how fully she experienced the extremes of joy and misery in her childhood, and again in her old age. It becomes clear that her sensitivity and imagination left few realms of life untouched.

In her first widely read novel, *The House of Mirth,* Wharton described the seal that Lily Bart used in her correspondence: a "flying" ship above the engraved word "Beyond." Perhaps the secret word Lawrence Selden planned to whisper to Lily—but could do so only after her death—was "Beyond." In Wharton's late story "Roman Fever," one of her most perfectly structured and often-anthologized works, she presents two middle-aged women who have known each other since childhood and have long assumed that they know everything about each other. Similarly, they even think that they can see nothing new in their travels because the most magnificent sights have become familiar to them. The close of the story shocks them with disclosures of events in their youthful days that changed their destiny and that of their children. Those who have re-read the story many times are still startled by the force and power of its compressed narrative as the women suddenly see beyond their familiar assumptions.

Similarly in the half-century since her death, Wharton scholars and readers who have watched her reputation grow beyond the level it had reached in her lifetime have been struck continually by new revelations about her work and life and have responded to "rediscoveries" of her greatness with new critical interpretations of her fiction and other writings. In her final years, Wharton looked forward to broadened revelations of life in spite of illness and grief. She wrote of her waking to view each day as an adventure and on the last page of *A Backward Glance* was able to say: "there are always new countries to see, new books to read (and, I hope, to write), a thousand little daily wonders to marvel at and rejoice in, and those magical moments when the mere discovery that 'the woodspurge has a cup of three' brings not despair but delight. The visible world is a daily miracle for those who have eyes and ears."

More than most authors, Wharton left much that remains alive—beyond her "mortal lease"—and her work and life continue to offer the promise of new insights and discoveries—even surprises—yet to come. Where may they arise? Perhaps in studies of her notable friendships; her avid thirst for travel; her intense interest in architecture, design, and landscape art; her explorations of Victorians (particularly George Eliot and George Meredith) or her admiration of Theodore Roosevelt; and her final praise of Walter de la Mare.

After publication of *The House of Mirth* Edith Wharton received recognition as an important writer throughout her life, and she maintained that reputation posthumously. Only in recent years, however, has her major significance emerged, not only as a highly proficient artist and an extraordinarily intelligent and sensitive interpreter of nineteenth- and early twentieth-century civilization, but as a writer remarkable for her achievement in many genres and for her comprehensive vision. Part, but not all, of this wider acclaim of Wharton during the last two decades has been the result of feminist recognition of her work and her persistent questioning of the role of women in both historical and contemporary American society—and sometimes in Europe and Africa. Although she presented problems, dramatized conflicts, and clarified issues of gender inequality and marriage, she did so through her art and imagination and avoided propagandizing for simple solutions to problems in the relationships between men and women, between generations, and between classes. Greater insights into her life and broader explorations of new facets of her writings have derived also, in part, from the publications of her collected short stories, of her biography by R. W. B. Lewis, and of her correspondence, *The Letters of Edith Wharton,* edited by R. W. B. Lewis and Nancy Lewis.

Cultivated readers before about 1960 knew Wharton chiefly for her indisputable masterpieces: *The House of Mirth, Ethan Frome,* and *The Age of Innocence.* They tended, however, to overlook her acute and extensive rendition of the problems of women in a patriarchal society; her extensive work in short fiction in the novella, the short story, and narratives concerning the supernatural; her travel books; her autobiography; her panoramic masterpiece, *The Custom of the Country;* her sympathetic rendition of the plight of the artist in *Hudson River Bracketed* and *The Gods Arrive;* and her satiric depiction of American life in the 1920s, particularly in *The Children* and *Twilight Sleep.*

Wharton's achievement is as varied and extensive as that of any American woman writer to the present time, and the critical work done on her in the last twenty years has irrefutably established her commanding position in American letters. Her many works gather resonance in the memory, and their significance enlarges upon each reconsideration of them. They reveal the manifold suggestiveness, the richness of nuance, and the symbolic implications that are the hallmarks of great literary achievement.

Notes and References

Chapter One

1. *A Backward Glance* (New York: Appleton-Century, 1934), 326. Hereafter cited in the text as *BG.*

2. R. W. B. Lewis, *Edith Wharton: A Biography* (New York: Harper & Row, 1975), 44–46.

3. Leon Edel, ed., *Henry James: The Future of the Novel* (New York: Vintage Books, 1956), 4.

4. *The Writing of Fiction* (New York: Scribner's, 1925), 119. Hereafter cited in the text as *WF.*

5. Helpful in the comparison of Wharton and James is R. P. Blackmur's introduction to *Henry James's "The Art of the Novel"* (New York: Scribner's, 1934), vii–xxix. He discusses in detail the themes and techniques that James considers in his prefaces and illustrates in his fiction.

6. *Catholic World* 75 (June 1902): 422–23; *Chicago Chronicles,* 20 April 1902; Sara Norton and M. A. DeWolfe Howe, eds., *Letters of Charles Eliot Norton,* vol. 2 (Boston: Cambridge Riverside Press, 1913), 319; Van Wyck Brooks, *The Confident Years* (New York: Dent, 1952), 288–89.

7. Information on the Fullerton affair is based mostly on Lewis, *Edith Wharton: A Biography,* and R. W. B. Lewis and Nancy Lewis, eds., *The Letters of Edith Wharton* (New York: Scribner's, 1988). Hereafter cited in the text as *Letters.* See Marion Mainwaring, "The Shock of Non-Recognition," *Times Literary Supplement,* 16–22 December 1988, 1394 and 1405, for a note on her unpublished data on the Wharton/Fullerton affair.

8. For descriptions of the manuscript journal called informally the Love Diary and titled by Wharton "The Life Apart," see Lewis, *Edith Wharton: A Biography,* 203–6, and Cynthia Griffin Wolff, *A Feast of Words* (New York: Oxford University Press, 1977), 146–51.

9. *Letters,* see dates from 1907 to 1910, pp. 127–225, passim.

10. Arline Golden, "Edith Wharton's Debt to Meredith in 'The Mortal Lease,' " *Yale University Library Gazette* 53:2 (October 1978): 100–8.

11. Information on Wharton's war service is based largely on Lewis, *Edith Wharton: A Biography.*

12. For further information on Wharton's wartime writing, see Alan Price, "Writing Home from the Front," *Edith Wharton Newsletter* (Fall 1988): 1–5, who compares the writing of Wharton and Dorothy Canfield Fisher, 1917–19. See also his "The Making of Edith Wharton's *The Book of the Homeless," Princeton University Library Chronicle* 47 (Autumn 1985): 5–23.

13. Information on the friendship of Wharton and Sinclair Lewis is available in William Rose Benet, "The Earlier Lewis," *Saturday Review Treasury* (New York: Simon & Schuster, 1957), 30–35; Robert L. Coard, "Edith Wharton's Influence on Sinclair Lewis," *Modern Fiction Studies* 31 (Autumn 1985): 511–27; Grace Hegger Lewis, *"With Love from Grace":Sinclair Lewis, 1912–25* (New York:Harcourt, 1955); Kenneth Rockwell, "From Society to Babbittry: Lewis's Debt to Edith Wharton," *Journal of the Central Mississippi Valley American Studies Association* (1960): 32–37; and Ellen Dupree, "Wharton, Lewis, and the Nobel Prize Address," *American Literature* 56 (May 1984): 262–70.

Chapter Two

1. *The House of Mirth* (New York: Scribner's, 1905), 515–16. Hereafter cited in the text as *HM*. Erskine Steele, "Fiction and Social Ethics," *South Atlantic Quarterly* 5, no. 3 (July 1906): 254–63.

2. Richard Poirier, "Edith Wharton, *The House of Mirth*," in *The American Novel*, ed. Wallace Stegner (New York: Basic Books, 1965), 117–32.

3. Walter Rideout, "Edith Wharton's *The House of Mirth*," in *Twelve Original Essays*, ed. Charles Shapiro (Detroit: 1958), 173; Geoffrey Walton, *Edith Wharton* (Teaneck, N.J.: Fairleigh Dickinson University Press, 1970), 59.

4. Blake Nevius, *Edith Wharton* (Berkeley: University of California Press, 1961), 59.

5. Recent critics who have analyzed the novel's connection with American economics at the turn of the century include Alan Price, "Lily Bart and Cary Meeber: Cultural Sisters," *American Literary Realism* 13 (Autumn 1980): 238–45; Wai-Chee Dimock, "Debasing Exchange: Edith Wharton's *The House of Mirth*," *PMLA* 100, no. 5 (October 1985); Robert Shulman, "Divided Selves and the Market Society: Politics and Psychology in *The House of Mirth*," *Perspectives on Contemporary Literature* 11 (1985): 10–19; Elizabeth Ammons, *Edith Wharton's Argument with America* (Athens: University of Georgia Press, 1980), 25–43.

6. Recent critics who relate the portrayal of beautiful women in this novel to the art of its time include Cathy Davidson, "Kept Women in *The House of Mirth*," *Markham Review* 9 (Fall 1979): 10–13; Judith Fetterly, "The Temptation to Be a Beautiful Object: Double Bind in *The House of Mirth*," *Studies in American Fiction* 5 (1977): 199–211; Joan Lidoff, "Another Sleeping Beauty: Narcissism in *The House of Mirth*," *American Quarterly* 32 (1980): 519–39; Frances Restuccia, "The Name of the Lily: Edith Wharton's Feminism(s)," *Contemporary Literature* 28 (Summer 1987): 223–38; Cynthia Griffin Wolff, "Lily Bart and the Beautiful Death," *American Literature* 46 (1974): 36–40, and revised in Wolff's *A Feast of Words*, 112–33; Judith Fryer, *Felicitous Space* (Chapel Hill: University of North Carolina Press, 1986), 75–82.

Chapter Three

1. *The Fruit of the Tree* (New York: Scribners, 1907), 292. Hereafter cited in the text as *FT*.

2. Judge Robert Grant a few weeks after publication of *The Fruit of the Tree* praised its structure. Wharton wrote that she had been discouraged and bewildered by critics who attacked what she considered to be the book's strong point and overlooked its weaknesses. See Lewis and Lewis, *Letters,* 123–25.

3. *The Reef* (New York: Scribner's, 1912), 106. Hereafter cited in the text as *TR*.

4. *The Letters of Henry James,* ed. Percy Lubbock, vol. 2 (London: Macmillan, 1920), 281–86.

5. A similar description of this hotel room near the train station appears in Wharton's poem "Terminus." Such autobiographical details led her friends to see her as identifying with Anna Leath and even with Sophy or Darrow in parts of *The Reef* because of the recent Fullerton affair and Teddy Wharton's affairs. She wrote in late 1912 to Bernard Berenson, "It's not me, though I thought it was when I was writing it" (Lewis and Lewis, *Letters,* 284). Near the close of the war, in thanking her editor, William Brownell, for praising *The Reef,* she wrote on 29 August 1918, "I put most of myself into that piece" (Wharton Archives, Amherst College; cited in Wolff, *A Feast of Words,* 218).

6. See Jean Gooder, "Unlocking Edith Wharton: An Introduction to *The Reef,*" *Cambridge Quarterly* 15, no. 1 (1986): 33–52; Moira Maynard, "Moral Integrity in *The Reef:* Justice to Anna Leath," *College Literature* 14 (Fall 1987): 285–95.

Chapter Four

1. Warner Berthoff, *The Ferment of Realism* (Cambridge: Cambridge University Press, 1981), 147.

2. Lewis, *Edith Wharton: A Biography,* 349–50.

3. Lewis and Lewis, *Letters,* 148; Lewis, *Edith Wharton: A Biography,* 141–142.

4. Henry James, "The New Novel," in *Notes on Novelists* (New York, 1914), 353–56.

5. Nevius, *Edith Wharton,* 158. For other views on Undine's strategies and goals, see Alan Price, "Dreiser's Cowperwood and Wharton's Undine Spragg: A Match Made in Spencer's Heaven," *Markham Review* 16 (Spring–Summer 1987): 37–39; Nancy Morrow, "Games and Conflict in Edith Wharton's *The Custom of the Country,*" *American Literary Realism* 17 (Spring 1984: 32–39; Alexandra Collins, "The Noyade of Marriage in Edith Wharton's *The Custom of the Country,*" *English Studies in Canada* 9 (June 1983): 197–212.

6. *The Custom of the Country* (New York: Scribner's, 1913), 266. Hereafter cited in the text as *CC*.

7. This same masseuse appears more than twenty years later in Wharton's "The Looking-Glass."

8. Walton, *Edith Wharton,* 108.

Chapter Five

1. *The Age of Innocence* (New York: Appleton, 1920), 170. Hereafter cited in the text as *AI.*

2. W. J. Stuckey, *The Pulitzer Prize Novels* (Norman: University of Oklahoma Press, 1966), 39–42.

3. Vernon Parrington, "Our Literary Aristocrat," *Pacific Review* (June 1921):157–60.

4. Nevius, *Edith Wharton,* 178.

5. Joseph Warren Beach, *The Twentieth-Century Novel* (New York: Century, 1932), 291–303.

6. See Louis O. Coxe, "What Edith Wharton Saw in Innocence," *New Republic,* 27 June 1955, 16–18; reprinted in Irving Howe, ed., *Edith Wharton: A Collection of Critical Essays* (Englewood Cliffs, N.J.: Prentice-Hall, 1962), 155–61. Emphasizes the irony of the conventional May Welland being the heroic character in the novel.

7. Viola Hopkins Winner, "The Ordering Style of *The Age of Innocence.*" *American Literature* 30 (November 1958): 345–57. In my analysis of Edith Wharton's imagery, I am indebted to Winner's study. See also James A. Robinson, "Psychological Determinism in *The Age of Innocence,*" *Markham Review* 5 (1975): 1–5. Places Archer's moments of greatest conflict in an anthropological context.

Chapter Six

1. *The Touchstone* (New York: Scribner's, 1900), 116.

2. Introduction to *Ethan Frome,* Modern Students Library Edition (New York: Charles Scribner's Sons, 1922), v. Hereafter *Ethan Frome* is cited in the text as *EF.*

3. Percy Lubbock, *Portrait of Edith Wharton* (London: Jonathan Cape, 1947), 130–31, recounts that after she passed a neglected, unpainted farmhouse she stopped at the meeting house to spend an hour alone trying to imagine what life would be like for people living in that house.

4. See, for instance, John Crowe Ransom, "Characters and Character," *American Review* (January 1936): 271–75; Bernard DeVoto, Introduction to *Ethan Frome* (New York: Scribner, 1938), xviii; Lionel Trilling, "The Morality of Inertia," *A Gathering of Fugitives* (Boston: Beacon Press, 1956), 31–40.

5. Important interpretations representing current ideas on *Ethan Frome* include: Elizabeth Ammons, "Edith Wharton's *Ethan Frome* and the Question of Meaning," *Studies in American Fiction* (1978): 127–40; Jean Blackall, "The Sledding Accident in *Ethan Frome,*" *Studies in Short Fiction* 21 (Spring 1984): 145–46;

David Eggenschwiler, "The Ordered Disorder of *Ethan Frome,*" *Studies in the Novel* 9 (Fall 1977): 237–46; R. B. Hovey, "*Ethan Frome:* A Controversy about Modernizing It," *American Literary Realism* 19 (Fall 1986): 4–20; and Orlene Murad, "Edith Wharton and *Ethan Frome,*" *Modern Language Studies* 13 (Summer 1983): 90–103.

6. For some sharply differing interpretations of *Summer* in criticism of the 1980s, see John Crowley, "The Unmastered Streak: Feminist Themes in Wharton's *Summer,*" *American Literary Realism* 15 (Spring 1982): 86–96; Linda Morante, "The Desolation of Charity Royall: Imagery in Edith Wharton's *Summer,*" *Colby Library Quarterly* 18 (December 1982): 241–48; Nancy A. Walker, " 'Seduced and Abandoned': Convention and Reality in Edith Wharton's *Summer,*" *Studies in American Fiction* 11 (Spring 1983): 107–14; Carol Wershoven, "The Divided Conflict of Edith Wharton's *Summer,*" *Colby Library Quarterly* 21 (March 1985): 5–10; Barbara Anne White, *Growing Up Female: Adolescent Girlhood in American Fiction* (Westport, Conn.: Greenwood Press, 1985), 47–64; and Barbara Anne White, "Edith Wharton's *Summer* and Women's Fiction," *Essays in Literature* 2 (Fall 1984): 223–35.

7. Judith Saunders, "Ironic Reversal in Edith Wharton's *Bunner Sisters,*" *Studies in Short Fiction* 14 (Summer 1977):241–45.

8. The date after the title of a story refers to its first appearance in a collection; for stories Wharton chose not to include in a book the date refers to its publication in a magazine.

9. In R. W. B. Lewis, ed., *The Collected Stories of Edith Wharton,* vol. 1 (New York: Charles Scribner's Sons, 1968), xxvi.

Chapter Seven

1. "Profile of Edith Wharton," *New York Herald Tribune,* European Edition, 16 November 1936.

2. Letter dated 8 June 1925 in F. Scott Fitzgerald, *The Crack-Up,* ed. Edmund Wilson (New York: J. Laughlin, 1945), 309.

3. Lubbock, *Portrait of Edith Wharton,* 200–1.

4. "The Great American Novel," *Yale Review* 16 (1927): 655.

5. *Fighting France* (New York: Scribner's, 1915), 204.

6. Frederick J. Hoffman, *The Twenties* (New York: Viking Press 1955), 47–51.

7. Edmund Wilson, "*Twilight Sleep,*" *New Republic* 51 (1927): 78.

8. Ibid.

9. *Twilight Sleep* (New York: Appleton, 1927), 253. Hereafter cited in the text as *TS.*

10. Q. D. Leavis, "Henry James's Heiress: The Importance of Edith Wharton," *Scrutiny,* December 1938, 269–70.

11. *The Children* (New York: Appleton, 1928), 2. Hereafter cited in the text as *TC.*

Chapter Eight

1. Nevius, *Edith Wharton,* 20.

2. *The Gods Arrive* (New York: Appleton, 1932), 37. Hereafter cited in the text as *GA.*

3. *Hudson River Bracketed* (New York: Appleton, 1929), 171. Hereafter cited in the text as *HRB.*

4. Gaillard Lapsley, "A Note on *The Buccaneers,*" in *The Buccaneers* (New York: Appleton-Century, 1938), 360. Hereafter cited in the text as *TB.*

5. Louis Auchincloss, "Edith Wharton and Her New Yorks," *Partisan Review* 18 (1951): 419.

6. Walton, *Edith Wharton,* 177.

7. Ibid., 184.

Selected Bibliography

Primary Works

Novels

The Age of Innocence. New York: Appleton, 1920.
The Buccaneers. New York: Appleton-Century, 1938.
The Children. New York: Appleton, 1928.
The Custom of the Country. New York: Scribner's, 1913.
The Fruit of the Tree. New York: Scribner's, 1907.
The Glimpses of the Moon. New York: Appleton, 1932.
The Gods Arrive. New York: Appleton, 1932.
The House of Mirth. New York: Scribner's, 1905.
Hudson River Bracketed. New York: Appleton, 1929.
The Mother's Recompense. New York: Appleton, 1925.
The Reef. New York: Scribner's, 1912.
A Son at the Front. New York: Scribner's, 1923.
Twilight Sleep. New York: Appleton, 1927.
The Valley of Decision. 2 vols. New York: Scribner's, 1902.

Novellas

Bunner Sisters. In *Xingu and Other Stories.* New York: Scribner's, 1916.
Ethan Frome. New York: Scribner's, 1911.
Fast and Loose. Pseudonym, David Olivieri. Edited by Viola Hopkins Winner. Charlottesville: University Press of Virginia, 1977.
Her Son. In *Human Nature.* New York: Appleton, 1933.
Madame de Treymes. New York: Scribner's, 1907.
The Marne. New York: Appleton, 1918.
Old New York. Four novellas in separate volumes. (*False Dawn, The Old Maid, The Spark, New Year's Day*). New York: Scribner's, 1924.
Sanctuary. New York: Scribner's, 1903.
Summer. New York: Appleton, 1917.
The Touchstone. New York: Scribner's, 1900.

Story Collections

Certain People. New York: Appleton, 1930.
Crucial Instances. New York: Scribner's, 1901.

The Descent of Man and Other Stories. New York: Scribner's, 1904.
Ghosts. New York: Appleton-Century, 1937.
The Greater Inclination. New York: Scribner's, 1899.
Here and Beyond. New York: Appleton, 1926.
The Hermit and the Wild Woman and Other Stories. New York: Scribner's, 1908.
Human Nature. New York: Appleton, 1933.
Tales of Men and Ghosts. New York: Scribner's, 1910.
The World Over. New York: Appleton-Century, 1936.
Xingu and Other Stories. New York: Scribner's, 1916.
The Collected Short Stories of Edith Wharton. 2 vols. Edited with introduction by
    R. W. B. Lewis. Boston: Houghton Mifflin, 1971.

Nonfiction

A Backward Glance. New York: Appleton-Century, 1934.
The Decoration of Houses (with Ogden Codman, Jr.). New York: Scribner's, 1891.
Fighting France. New York: Scribner's, 1915.
French Ways and Their Meaning. New York: Appleton, 1919.
In Morocco. New York: Scribner's, 1920.
Italian Backgrounds. New York: Scribner's, 1905.
Italian Villas and Their Gardens. New York: Century, 1904.
A Motor-Flight through France. New York: Scribner's, 1908.
The Writing of Fiction. New York: Scribner's, 1925.

Poetry

Artemis to Actaeon and Other Verse. New York: Scribner's, 1909.
Twelve Poems. London: The Medici Society, 1926.
Verses. Newport, Rhode Island: C. E. Hammett, 1878.

Secondary Works

Books

Ammons, Elizabeth. *Edith Wharton's Argument with America*. Athens: Univer-
    sity of Georgia Press, 1980. Close integration of feminist/political theory with
    detailed study of Wharton's texts.
Auchincloss, Louis. *Edith Wharton: A Woman in Her Time*. New York: Viking,
    1971. Criticism, biography, and many good photographs.
Bell, Millicent. *Edith Wharton and Henry James: The Story of Their Friendship*.
    New York: George Braziller, 1965. Uses correspondence of both writers in es-
    tablishing their relationship.

Edel, Leon. *Henry James, the Master: 1901–1916.* New York: Lippincott, 1972. Includes details of the friendship of James and Wharton.

Fryer, Judith. *Felicitous Space.* Chapel Hill: University of North Carolina Press, 1986. Merges theories of literary and art criticism in interpreting Wharton and Cather.

Lewis, R. W. B. *Edith Wharton: A Biography.* New York: Harper & Row, 1975. Biography and criticism.

Lewis, R. W. B., and Nancy Lewis, eds. *Collected Letters of Edith Wharton.* New York: Scribner's, 1989. Four hundred letters with valuable introductions and notes.

Lindberg, Gary. *Edith Wharton and the Novel of Manners.* Charlottesville: University Press of Virginia, 1975 Focuses on society and manners; major novels.

Lubbock, Percy. *Portrait of Edith Wharton.* London: Jonathan Cape, 1947. Established negative images of Wharton; by a former friend.

Nevius, Blake. *Edith Wharton: A Study of Her Fiction.* Berkeley: University of California Press, 1953. Discounts Lubbock's evaluation; excellent critiques.

Rae, Catherine. *Edith Wharton's New York Quartet.* Lanham, Md.: University Press of America, 1984. Criticism of the novellas in *Old New York.*

Walton, Geoffrey. *Edith Wharton: A Critical Interpretation.* Teaneck, N.J.: Fairleigh Dickinson University Press, 1970. Detailed and judicious criticism.

Wershoven, Carol. *The Female Intruder in the Novels of Edith Wharton.* Rutherford, N.J.: Fairleigh Dickinson University Press, 1982. Argues that Wharton's heroines as "outsiders" bring questioning of old societies and values.

Wolff, Cynthia Griffin. *A Feast of Words: The Triumph of Edith Wharton.* New York: Oxford University Press, 1977. Psychological biography and criticism.

Bibliographies

Bendixen, Alfred. "A Guide to Wharton Criticism, 1974–1983." *Edith Wharton Newsletter* 2, no. 2 (Fall 1985): 1–8. "Recent Wharton Studies: A Bibliographic Essay." *Edith Wharton Newsletter* 3, no. 2 (Fall 1986): 5,8. "Wharton Studies, 1986–1987: A Bibliographic Essay." *Edith Wharton Newsletter* 5, no. 1 (Spring 1988): 5–8, 10.

Lauer, Kristin O., and Margaret P. Murray. *Edith Wharton: An Annotated Secondary Bibliography.* New York and London: Garland Publishing, 1990.

Springer, Marlene. *Edith Wharton and Kate Chopin: A Reference Guide.* Boston: G. K. Hall, 1976. Annotates works by and about Wharton to 1973, the beginning date of a series of bibliographies in *Edith Wharton Newsletter.*

Tuttleton, James W. "Edith Wharton: An Essay in Bibliography." *Resources for American Literary Study,* Fall 1973, 163–202. Annotations of essays and reviews; criticism; some listing of unpublished materials.

Essay Collections

Bendixen, Alfred, and Annette Zilversmit, eds. *New Essays on Edith Wharton.* New York: Garland Press, 1990. Almost all essays previously unprinted.

Bloom, Harold, ed. *Edith Wharton.* Modern Critical Views Series. New York: Chelsea House, 1986. Reprints influential criticism.

College Literature (Fall 1987). Special issue on Edith Wharton containing nine of the sixty-two papers presented at June 1987 conference at The Mount.

Howe, Irving, ed. *Edith Wharton: A Collection of Critical Essays.* Englewood Cliffs, N.J.: Prentice-Hall, 1962. Influential in revival of interest in Wharton.

Index

About the Author

Margaret B. McDowell is professor of rhetoric and women's studies at the University of Iowa. A summa cum laude graduate of Coe College, she received the M.A. in creative writing and the Ph.D. in English from the University of Iowa. In the last fifteen years her writing has been devoted mostly to critical studies of British and American women writers. She is also the author of *Carson McCullers* (1980).